WITHDRAWN

D1361943

ALDOUS HUXLEY

*

Along the Road

By ALDOUS HUXLEY

Novels
CROME YELLOW
ANTIC HAY
THOSE BARREN LEAVES
POINT COUNTER POINT *
BRAVE NEW WORLD
EYELESS IN GAZA
AFTER MANY A SUMMER
TIME MUST HAVE A STOP

Short Stories
LIMBO *
MORTAL COILS
LITTLE MEXICAN
TWO OR THREE GRACES
BRIEF CANDLES

Biography
GREY EMINENCE

Essays and Belles Lettres
ON THE MARGIN *
ALONG THE ROAD
PROPER STUDIES
DO WHAT YOU WILL
MUSIC AT NIGHT &
VULGARITY IN LITERATURE
TEXTS AND PRETEXTS (Anthology)
THE OLIVE TREE *
ENDS AND MEANS (An Enquiry
into the Nature of Ideals) *
THE ART OF SEEING
THE PERENNIAL PHILOSOPHY
SCIENCE, LIBERTY AND PEACE

Travel
JESTING PILATE (Illustrated) *
BEYOND THE MEXIQUE BAY (Illustrated)

Poetry and Drama
VERSES AND A COMEDY *
(including early poems, Leda, The Cicadas
and The World of Light, a Comedy)

* Issued in this Collected Edition

ALDOUS HUXLEY

Along the Road

*Notes and Essays of
a Tourist*

1948
Chatto & Windus
LONDON

PUBLISHED BY

Chatto & Windus

LONDON

*

Oxford University Press

TORONTO

Applications regarding translation rights in any
work by Aldous Huxley should be addressed
to Chatto & Windus, 40 William IV Street,
London, W.C. 2

FIRST PUBLISHED 1925
FIRST ISSUED IN THIS COLLECTED
EDITION 1948
PRINTED IN GREAT BRITAIN
ALL RIGHTS RESERVED

CONTENTS

∽

vii

44405

ALONG THE ROAD

PART IV
BY THE WAY

Part 1

TRAVEL IN GENERAL

A

WHY NOT STAY AT HOME?

Some people travel on business, some in search of health. But it is neither the sickly nor the men of affairs who fill the Grand Hotels and the pockets of their proprietors. It is those who travel 'for pleasure,' as the phrase goes. What Epicurus, who never travelled except when he was banished, sought in his own garden, our tourists seek abroad. And do they find their happiness? Those who frequent the places where they resort must often find this question, with a tentative answer in the negative, fairly forced upon them. For tourists are, in the main, a very gloomy-looking tribe. I have seen much brighter faces at a funeral than in the Piazza of St. Mark's. Only when they can band together and pretend, for a brief, precarious hour, that they are at home, do the majority of tourists look really happy. One wonders why they come abroad.

The fact is that very few travellers really like travelling. If they go to the trouble and expense of travelling, it is not so much from curiosity, for fun, or because they like to see things beautiful and strange, as out of a kind of snobbery. People travel for the same reason as they collect works of art : because the best people do it. To have been to certain spots on the earth's surface is socially correct ; and having been there, one is superior to those who have not. Moreover, travelling gives one something to talk about when one gets home. The subjects of conversation are not so numerous that one can neglect an opportunity of adding to one's store.

To justify this snobbery, a series of myths has gradually been elaborated. The places which it is socially smart to have visited are aureoled with glamour, till they are made to appear, for those who have not been there, like so many fabled Babylons or Bagdads. Those who have travelled have a personal interest in cultivating and disseminating these fables. For if Paris and Monte Carlo are really so marvellous as it is generally supposed, by the inhabitants of Bradford or Milwaukee, of Tomsk and Bergen, that they are—why, then, the merit of the travellers who have actually visited these places is the greater, and their superiority over the stay-at-homes the more enormous. It is for this reason (and because they pay the hotel proprietors and the steamship companies) that the fables are studiously kept alive.

Few things are more pathetic than the spec-

4

tacle of inexperienced travellers, brought up on these myths, desperately doing their best to make external reality square with fable. It is for the sake of the myths and, less consciously, in the name of snobbery that they left their homes ; to admit disappointment in the reality would be to admit their own foolishness in having believed the fables and would detract from their merit in having undertaken the pilgrimage. Out of the hundreds of thousands of Anglo-Saxons who frequent the night-clubs and dancing-saloons of Paris, there are a good many, no doubt, who genuinely like that sort of thing. But there are also very many who do not. In their hearts, secretly, they are bored and a little disgusted. But they have been brought up to believe in a fabulous ' Gay Paree,' where everything is deliriously exciting and where alone it is possible to see what is technically known as Life. Conscientiously, therefore, they strive, when they come to Paris, to be gay. Night after night the dance halls and the bordellos are thronged by serious young compatriots of Emerson and Matthew Arnold, earnestly engaged in trying to see life, neither very steadily nor whole, through the ever-thickening mists of Heidsieck and Roederer.

Still more courageously determined are their female companions ; for they, mostly (unless they are extremely ' modern '), have not the Roederer to assist them in finding Paris gay. The saddest sight I ever saw was in a Montmartre *boîte* at about five o'clock of an autumn morning. At a table in a corner of the hall sat three young American girls, quite unattended, adventurously seeing life by themselves. In front of them, on the table, stood the regulation bottles of champagne ; but for preference—perhaps on principle —they were sipping lemonade. The jazz band played on monotonously ; the tired drummer nodded over his drums, the saxophonist yawned into his saxophone. In couples, in staggering groups, the guests departed. But grimly, indomitably, in spite of their fatigue, in spite of the boredom which so clearly expressed itself on their charming and ingenuous faces, the three young girls sat on. They were still there when I left at sunrise. What stories, I reflected, they would tell when they got home again ! And how envious they would make their untravelled friends. ' Paris is just wonderful. . . .'

To the Parisians, the fable brings in several hundred milliards of good money. They give it a generous publicity ; business is business. But

6

if I were the manager of a Montmartre dancing-saloon, I think I should tell my waiters to act their gay parts with a little more conviction. ' My men,' I should say to them, ' you ought to look as though you believed in the fable out of which we make our living. Smile, be merry. Your present expression, which is a mingling of weariness, disgusted contempt for your clients and cynical rapacity, is not inspiring. One day the clients might be sober enough to notice it. And where should we be then ? '

But Paris and Monte Carlo are not the only resorts of pilgrimage. There are also Rome and Florence. There are picture galleries, churches and ruins as well as shops and casinos. And the snobbery which decrees that one must like Art—or, to be more accurate, that one should have visited the places where Art is to be seen—is almost as tyrannous as that which bids one visit the places where one can see Life.

All of us are more or less interested in Life—even in that rather smelly slice of it that is to be found in Montmartre. But a taste for Art—or at any rate the sort of art that is found in galleries and churches—is by no means universal. Hence the case of the poor tourists who, from motives of snobbery, visit Rome and Florence, is even more

7

pathetic than the case of those who repair for the same reasons to Paris and Monte Carlo. Tourists ' doing ' a church wear a mask of dutiful interest ; but what lassitude, what utter weariness of spirit looks out, too often, at their eyes ! And the weariness is felt, within, still more acutely because, precisely, of the necessity of simulating this rapt attentiveness, of even going hypocritically into raptures over the things that are starred in the Baedeker. There come moments when flesh and blood can stand the strain no longer. Philistinism absolutely refuses to pay the tribute it owes to taste. Exasperated and defiant, the tourist swears that he won't so much as put his nose inside another church, preferring to spend his days in the lounge of the hotel, reading the continental *Daily Mail*.

I remember witnessing one of these rebellions at Venice. A motor boat company was advertising afternoon excursions to the island of Torcello. We booked our seats and at the appointed time set off, in company with seven or eight other tourists. Romantic in its desolation, Torcello rose out of the lagoon. The boatmen drew up at the side of a mouldering jetty. A quarter of a mile away, through the fields, stood the church. It contains some of the most beautiful mosaics in

8

Italy. We climbed on shore—all of us with the exception of one strong-minded American couple who, on learning that the object of interest on this island was only another church, decided to remain comfortably seated in the boat till the rest of the party should return. I admired them for their firmness and their honesty. But at the same time, it seemed to me rather a melancholy thing that they should have come all this way and spent all that money, merely for the pleasure of sitting in a motor boat tied to a rotting wharf. And then they were only at Venice. Their Italian ordeal had hardly begun. Padua, Ferrara, Ravenna, Bologna, Florence, Siena, Perugia, Assisi and Rome, with all their innumerable churches and pictures, had still to be looked at, before—the blessed goal of Naples finally reached —they could be permitted to take the liner home again across the Atlantic. Poor slaves, I thought ; and of how exacting a master !

We call such people travellers because they do not stay at home. But they are not genuine travellers, not travellers born. For they travel, not for travelling's sake, but for convention's. They set out, nourished on fables and fantastical hopes, to return, whether they avow it or not, disappointed. Their interest in the real and

9

actual being insufficiently lively, they hanker after mythology, and the facts, however curious, beautiful and varied, are a disillusionment. It is only the society of their fellow-tourists, with whom they conspire, every now and then, to make a little oasis of home in the foreign wilderness, coupled with the consciousness of a social duty done, that keeps them even moderately cheerful in the face of the depressing facts of travel.

Your genuine traveller, on the other hand, is so much interested in real things that he does not find it necessary to believe in fables. He is insatiably curious, he loves what is unfamiliar for the sake of its unfamiliarity, he takes pleasure in every manifestation of beauty. It would be absurd, of course, to say that he is never bored. For it is practically impossible to travel without being sometimes bored. For the tourist, a large part of almost every day is necessarily empty. Much time, to begin with, must be spent in merely getting from place to place. And when the sights have been seen, the sight-seer finds himself physically weary and with nothing particular to do. At home, among one's regular occupations, one is never bored. Ennui is essentially a holiday feeling. (Is it not the chronic disease

of the leisured ?)   It is for that very reason that
your true traveller finds boredom rather agreeable than painful.   It is the symbol of his liberty
—his excessive freedom.   He accepts his boredom, when it comes, not merely philosophically,
but almost with pleasure.

For the born traveller, travelling is a besetting
vice.   Like other vices it is imperious, demand-
ing its victim's time, money, energy and the
sacrifice of his comfort.   It claims ; and the born
traveller gives, willingly, even eagerly.   Most
vices, it may be added parenthetically, demand
considerable self-sacrifices.   There is no greater
mistake than to suppose that a vicious life is a life
of uninterrupted pleasure.   It is a life almost as
wearisome and painful—if strenuously led—as
Christian's in *The Pilgrim's Progress*.   The chief
difference between Christian and the vicious man
is that the first gets something out of his hardships
—gets it here and now in the shape of a certain
spiritual well-being, to say nothing of what he
may get in that sadly problematical Jerusalem
beyond the river—while the second gets nothing,
except, perhaps, gout and general paralysis of the
insane.

The vice of travelling, it is true, does not necessarily bring with it these two particular diseases ;

11

SALEM COLLEGE LIBRARY
Winston-Salem, North Carolina

nor indeed any diseases at all, unless your wanderings take you as far as the tropics.   No bodily
diseases ; for travelling is not a vice of the body
(which it mortifies) but of the mind.   Your
traveller-for-travelling's-sake is like your desultory reader—a man addicted to mental self-in-
dulgence.

Like all other vicious men, the reader and the
traveller have a whole armoury of justifications
with which to defend themselves.   Reading and
travelling, they say, broaden the mind, stimulate
imagination, are a liberal education.   And so on.
These are specious arguments ; but nobody is
very much impressed by them.   For though it
may be quite true that, for certain people, desultory reading and aimless travelling are richly
educative, it is not for that reason that most true
readers and travellers born indulge their tastes.
We read and travel, not that we may broaden and
enrich our minds, but that we may pleasantly
forget they exist.   We love reading and travelling because they are the most delightful of all
the many substitutes for thought.   Sophisticated
and somewhat rarefied substitutes.   That is why
they are not every man's diversion.   The congenital reader or traveller is one of those more
fastidious spirits who cannot find the distractions

they require in betting, mah-jongg, drink, golf or fox-trots.

There exist a few, a very few, who travel and, for that matter, who read, with purpose and a definite system. This is a morally admirable class. And it is the class to which, in general, the people who achieve something in the world belong. Not always, however, by any means. For, alas, one may have a high purpose and a fine character, but no talent. Some of the most self-indulgent and aimless of travellers and readers have known how to profit by their vices. Desultory reading was Dr. Johnson's besetting sin ; he read every book that came under his hand and none to the end. And yet his achievement was not small. And there are frivolous travellers, like Beckford, who have gone about the world, indulging their wanton curiosity, to almost as good purpose. Virtue is its own reward ; but the grapes which talent knows how to pluck— are they not a little sour ?

With me, travelling is frankly a vice. The temptation to indulge in it is one which I find almost as hard to resist as the temptation to read promiscuously, omnivorously and without purpose. From time to time, it is true, I make a desperate resolution to mend my ways. I sketch out programmes of useful, serious reading ; I try to turn my rambling voyages into systematic tours through the history of art and civilization. But without much success. After a little I relapse into my old bad ways. Deplorable weakness ! I try to comfort myself with the hope that even my vices may be of some profit to me.

WANDER-BIRDS

FAIR-HAIRED, bare-headed, with faces burned darker than their hair, they trudge along the dusty roads. They wear shorts ; their Tyrolean knees are brown. Enormous boots, heavy with nails, click metallically over the flagstones of the churches into which, conscientious *Kunstforschers*, they penetrate. On their backs they carry knapsacks and in their hands, sometimes a stick, sometimes a stout umbrella ; I have seen them making the ascent of the Viale dei Colli at Florence with ice-axes. They are the wander-birds, and they come, as their name (so romantic and applied so unironically), their Schillerian name too manifestly proclaims, from Germany. Many of them have walked all the way, across the Alps from Berlin to Taranto and back, with no money, living on bread and water, sleeping in barns or by the roadside. Adventurous and hardy youths ! I feel the profoundest admiration for them. I even envy them, wishing that I possessed their energy, their hardiness. But I do not imitate them.

> 'The saints of old,' says the hymnologist, 'went up to Heaven
> With sorrow, toil and pain.
> Lord, unto us may strength be given
> To follow in the train.'

15

For me, I confess, even the train has become a means of travelling too inconvenient to be much employed. I would amend the last two lines of the hymn to, ' Lord, unto us may wealth be given to follow in the car.' The prayer has been granted—partially, at any rate ; for whether a ten-horse-power Citroën can really be called a car is questionable. Owners of Napiers, Vauxhalls, Delages or Voisins, would certainly deny it. I shall not argue the point. All I claim for the ten-horse-power Citroën is this : that it works. In a modest and unassuming way, not very rapidly, indeed, but steadily and reliably, it takes one about. This particular specimen has carried us a good many thousand miles over the roads of Italy, France, Belgium and Holland ; which, for all who are acquainted with those roads, is saying a good deal.

At this point, if I had any strength of mind, I should stop talking about Citroëns and return to higher themes. But the temptation of talking about cars, when one has a car, is quite irresistible. Before I bought a Citroën no subject had less interest for me ; none, now, has more. I can talk for hours about motors with other car-owners. And I am ruthlessly prepared to bore the non-motorist by talking interminably of this delightful subject even to him. I waste much precious time reading the motoring papers, study passionately the news from the racing tracks, gravely peruse technical lucubrations which I do not understand. It is a madness, but a delightful one.

The spiritual effects of being a car-owner are not, I notice, entirely beneficial. Introspection and the conversation of other motorists have shown me, indeed, that car-owning may have the worst effect on the character. To begin with every car-owner is a liar. He cannot tell the truth about his machine. He exaggerates his speed, the number of miles he goes to the gallon of petrol, his prowess as a hill climber. In the heat of conversation I myself have erred in this respect, more than once ; and even coolly, with malice aforethought, I have given utterance, on this subject, to frigid and calculated lies. They do not weigh very heavily on my conscience. I am no casuist, but it seems to me that a lie which one tells, expecting nobody to believe it, is venial. The motorist, like the fisherman, never really supposes that his vaunts will be believed. Myself, I have long ceased to give the slightest credit to anything my fellow-motorists may tell me. My last vestige of confidence was destroyed by the Belgian driver who told me that two hours were ample time to allow for the journey from Brussels to Ostend ; he himself, he declared, did it constantly and never took more. I trusted him and did not consult the road book. If I had, I should have found that the distance from Brussels to Ostend is something over seventy miles, that the road is cobbled all the way and badly cobbled at that, and that one has to pass through three large towns and about twenty villages. As it was we started late in the afternoon and were hopelessly benighted. Now, when motorists tell me how long it takes them to get from one place to another, I add on, according to their character, from thirty to sixty per cent. to the figure they mention. In this way I reach approximate truth.

Another horrible sin encouraged by the owning of an automobile, particularly of a small automobile, is envy. What bitter discontentment fills the mind of the 10 H.P. man as the 40 H.P. shoots silently past him ! How fiercely he loathes the owner of the larger machine ! What envy and covetousness possess him ! In a flat country one envies less than in a hilly. For on the flat even the little car can do quite creditably enough to keep up its owner's self-esteem. It is in a mountainous country, like Italy, where the roads are constantly running up to two or three thousand feet and down again, that the deadly sin of envy really flourishes. For there the little car must abjectly acknowledge its littleness. The superiority of 40 H.P. over 10 H.P. is only too painfully apparent. It was on the Mont Cenis that the cup of our humiliation flowed over and the blackest envy filled our souls. We had started from Turin. For the first thirty miles the road is perfectly flat. We rolled along it in very dashing style ; the smaller Fiats ate our dust. In front of us, like an immense uneven wall, the Alps rose suddenly out of the plain. Susa lies at the head of a long flat-bottomed valley that leads into the heart of the hills. You pass through the town and then, suddenly, without warning, the road begins to climb, steeply. It goes on climbing without respite for the next fifteen miles. The top of the pass is six thousand five hundred feet above the sea. The Citroën went into second and remained there ; slowly we puffed up the long ascent. We had gone about a mile, when we became aware of a noise coming up from the valley, a noise like the noise of massed machine-guns. It grew louder and louder. A minute later a huge red Alfa Romeo road racer, looking suspiciously like the machine that had just won the Grand Prix of Europe, roared past at a speed that cannot have been less than fifty miles an hour. It was evidently being driven by a genius ; for, looking up, we saw the scarlet monster negotiating turn after hairpin turn in the zigzag road above us without once abating its speed by a mile an hour. In another thirty seconds it was out of sight. The noise of it solemnly reverberated among the mountains, like thunder. Slowly we puffed on. Half an hour later we met the red terror descending ; round the corners it showed the same disregard for the elementary laws of dynamics as it had shown on the way up. We imagined that we had seen the last of it. But waiting at the Italian custom-house while the officer in charge examined our papers—a process which, as at all custom-houses, took a very long time—we heard, far off, a familiar sound. In a few minutes the sound became deafening. Like a huge red rocket, trailing behind it a cloud of smoke, the Alfa Romeo passed at the head of its white dust. ' They 're doing hill-climbing tests,' the soldier on guard explained. We set out once more. The custom-house is only half-way up the hill ; we had another three thousand feet or so before we reached the summit. Slowly, on second, we addressed ourselves to the ascent. We were only a mile from the custom-house, when, for the second time, we met the Alfa Romeo descending. It disappeared, carrying with it a load of hatred, envy and mixed uncharitableness of every variety.

The road mounted and mounted. We passed through the region of pine woods. Around and above us, now, the slopes were bare ; quite close, among the nearer summits, across the valley, were patches of snow. For all that the season was summer, the air was uncommonly sharp and nipping. A wind blew ; in the shade it was positively cold. But that did not prevent the car from boiling.

The hospice and the hotels of the Mont Cenis stand on the shores of a lake in the middle of a little plateau that lies, a miracle of flatness amid the surrounding perpendicularity. Towards the Italian side this shelf among the hills ends abruptly in what is nearly a precipice. For the last four or five hundred feet the road leading up to it is terraced out of the rock and rises with uncommon steepness. We were half-way up these final zigzags, when all at once, bursting with a roar round the corner of a bluff that had muffled the sound of its approach, the scarlet Alfa Romeo appeared at the bottom of the precipice up which we were painfully zigzagging. It came up after us, like a wild beast pursuing its prey, bellowing. Just as we reached the top, the monster overhauled us, passed and went racing across the plain. Our humiliation was complete. Envy and discontent boiled up within us, like the water boiling in the radiator of our miserable little machine. 'If only,' we said, 'if only we had a real car. . . .' We longed to exchange the passion of envy for the equally malignant and un-Christian passions of pride and contempt, to be those who pass exultantly instead of those who are passed. 'Yea, also the heart of the sons of men is full of evil, and madness is in their heart while they live, and after that they go to the dead.' When we reached the hotel, the Alfa Romeo had turned round and was just preparing to begin its third descent. 'It's an ugly-looking car,' we said.

Such are the moral consequences of being the owner of a small car. We tried to reason with ourselves. 'After all,' we said, 'this little machine has done good service. It has taken us over bad roads, up and down enormous hills, through a variety of countries. It has taken us, not merely through space, across the face of the map, but through time—from epoch to epoch—

22

through art, through many languages and cus-
toms, through philology and anthropology. It
has been the instrument of great and varied
pleasures. It costs little, behaves well, its habits
are as regular as those of Immanuel Kant. In its
unpretentious way it is a model of virtue.' All
this we said, and much more ; and it was comforting. But in the bottom of our hearts envy
and discontent still lurked, like coiled serpents,
ready to raise their heads the very next time that
forty horses should pass us on a hill.

It may be objected that the small-car owner is
not alone in envying. The wander-birds doing
their four miles an hour, sweating, up the dusty
hill, must envy indiscriminately both the ten and
the forty horse-power man. True, some of them
probably do. But it must not be forgotten that
there are pedestrians who walk because they
genuinely prefer walking to being carried effortlessly along by a machine. In my youth I used
to try to pretend that I preferred walking to other
means of locomotion. But I soon found that it
was not true. For a little time I was one of those
hypocrites of country heartiness (and they are
quite numerous) who tramp and drink ale in little
inns, because it is the right thing to do. In the
end, however, I frankly admitted to myself and

to other people that I was not one of nature's walkers, that I did not like hearty exercise and discomfort, and did not mean any longer to pretend that I did. But I still have the greatest respect for those who do, and I consider that they are probably a superior type of humanity to the idle and comfort-loving breed predominant at the present time. One of the great charms of mechanical progress is that it allows us to do everything quickly, easily and comfortably. This is very agreeable ; but I doubt whether it is, morally speaking, very healthy. It is not even very healthy for the body. It is in the civilized countries, where human beings eat most and take least exercise, that cancer is most prevalent. The disease spreads with every fresh expansion of Henry Ford's factories.

None the less I prefer to follow in the car. To the wander-birds whom we pass on our way, I take off my hat. It is a mark of my sincere esteem. But inwardly I repeat to myself the words of the Abbot in the *Canterbury Tales* : 'Let Austin have his swink to him reserved.'

I COULD give many excellent reasons for my dislike of large dinner-parties, soirées, crushes, routs, conversazioni and balls. Life is not long enough and they waste precious time ; the game is not worth the candle. Casual social intercourse is like dram-drinking, a mere stimulant that whips the nerves but does not nourish. And so on. These are respectable contentions and all quite true. And they have certainly had weight with me. But the final argument against large assemblages and in favour of solitude and the small intimate gathering has been, in my case, of a more personal character. It has appealed, not to my reason, but my vanity. The fact is that I do not shine in large assemblies ; indeed, I scarcely glimmer. And to be dim and conscious of one's dimness is humiliating.

This incapacity to be bright in company is due entirely to my excessive curiosity. I cannot listen to what my interlocutor is saying or think of anything to say in answer to him, because I cannot help listening to the conversations being carried on by everybody else within earshot. My interlocutor, for example, is saying something very intelligent about Henry James and is obviously expecting me, when he has done, to make some smart or subtle comment. But the two women on my left are telling scandalous stories about a person I know. The man with the loud voice at the other side of the room is discussing the merits of different motor cars. The science student by the fireplace is talking about the quantum theory. The distinguished Irish lawyer is telling anecdotes in his inimitable professional manner. Behind me a youth and maiden are exchanging views on love, while from the group in the far corner I hear an occasional phrase which tells me that they are talking politics. An invincible curiosity possesses me, I long to hear exactly what each is saying. Scandal, motors, quanta, Irish bulls, love and politics seem to me incomparably more interesting than Henry James ; and each of these is at the same time more interesting than all the others. Inquisitiveness flutters hopelessly this way and that, like a bird in a glass house. And the net result is that, not hearing what he says and being too much distracted to answer coherently, I make myself appear an idiot to my interlocutor, while the very number of my illicit curiosities renders it impossible for me to satisfy any single one of them.

But this excessive and promiscuous inquisitiveness, so fatal to a man who desires to mix in society, is a valuable asset to the one who merely looks on, without participating in the actions of his fellows.

For the traveller, who is compelled, whether he likes to or not, to pose as the detached on-looker, inquisitiveness is nothing less than a necessity. Ennui, says Baudelaire, 'is *fruit de la morne incuriosité.*' The tourist who has no curiosity is doomed to boredom.

There are few pleasanter diversions than to sit in cafés or restaurants or the third-class carriages of railway trains, looking at one's neighbours and listening (without attempting to enter into conversation) to such scraps of their talk as are wafted across the intervening space. From their appearance, from what they say, one reconstructs in the imagination the whole character, the complete life history. Given the single fossil bone, one fancifully builds up the whole diplodocus. It is an excellent game. But it must be played discreetly. Too open a curiosity is apt to be resented. One must look and listen without appearing to be aware of anything. If the game is played by two people, comments should always be made in some language other than that of the country in which the game is played. But perhaps the most important rule of the game is that which forbids one, except in the most extraordinary cases, to make any effort to get to know the objects of one's curiosity.

For, alas, the objects of one's curiosity prove, once one has made their acquaintance, to be, almost invariably, quite unworthy of any further interest. It is possible at a distance to feel the most lively curiosity about a season-ticket holder from Surbiton. His bald head is so shiny ; he has such a funny waxed moustache ; he gets so red in the face when he talks to his friends about the socialists ; he laughs with such loud unpleasant gusto when one of them tells a dirty story ; he sweats so profusely when it is hot ; he holds forth so knowledgeably about roses; and his sister lives at Birmingham ; his son has just won a prize for mathematics at school. At long range all this is fascinating ; it stimulates the imagination. One loves the little man ; he is wonderful, charming, a real slice of life. But make his acquaintance. . . . From that day forth you take pains to travel in another compartment.

How delightful, how queer and fantastic people are, at a distance ! When I think of the number of fascinating men and women I have never known (only seen and momentarily listened to) I am astonished. I can remember hundreds of them. My favourites, I am inclined to think, were those male and female post-office clerks who lived *en pension* at the little hotel at Ambérieu where once I stayed for a week or so, finishing a book. They were fascinating. There was the oldish man, who always came in late for dinner, wearing a cap—a grim, taciturn fellow he was ; there was the very young boy, not at all grim, but silent out of pure shyness ; there was the very bright, lively, meridional fellow, who made jokes all the time and flirtatiously teased the young ladies ; and the three young ladies, one ugly but tolerably lively, one rather pretty but limp and chlorotic, and the third so full of attractive vitality that she compelled one to think her pretty—such rolling black eyes, such a smile, such a voice, so witty ! The shy young man gazed like a calf, blushed when she looked at him, smiled oxishly when she talked, and forgot to eat his dinner. Her presence thawed the grim and grizzled man and roused the meridional to yet higher flights. And her superiority was so enormous that the ugly girl and the chlorotic girl were not in the least jealous, but worshipped her. It is absurd to be jealous of the gods.

How I adored that party ! With what passionate interest I overlooked them from my table in the little dining-room ! How attentively I eavesdropped ! I learned where they had spent their holidays, which of them had been to Paris, where their relations lived, what they thought of the postmaster of Ambérieu, and a host of other things, all wonderfully interesting and exciting. But not for the world would I have made their acquaintance. The landlady offered to introduce me ; but I declined the honour. I am afraid she thought me a snob ; she was proud of her pensionnaires. It was impossible for me to explain that my reluctance to know them was due to the fact that I loved them even more than she did. To know them would have spoilt everything. From wonderful and mysterious beings, they would have degenerated into six rather dull and pathetic little employés, condemned to pass their lives drearily in a small provincial town.

And then there were the millionaires at Padua. How much we enjoyed those ! It was the waiter who told us they were plutocrats. In the restaurant of the Hotel Storione at Padua there is one special table, it appears, reserved for millionaires. Four or five of them lunched there regularly every day while we were in the hotel. Superb figures they were, and wonderfully in character like millionaires in an Italian film. In an American film, of course, the type is very different. A Hollywood millionaire is a strong, silent man, clean-shaven, with a face either like a hatchet or an uncooked muffin. These, on the contrary, had tremendous beards, talked a great deal, were over-dressed and wore white gloves. They looked like a little party of Bluebeards.

Another of my remembered favourites is the siren we saw at the Ristorante Centrale at Genoa. She sat at a neighbouring table with four men, all desperately in love with her, talking, one could see by the way they listened and laughed, like all the heroines of Congreve rolled into one. One of the men was a Turk and had to have recourse periodically to the interpreter, without whose aid the majority of diners in that polyglot restaurant would be unable to order their macaroni. One —he was old and paid for the dinner—must have been her husband or her lover. Poor fellow, he looked rather glum sometimes, when she addressed herself too fascinatingly to the Turk, who was her principal victim, or one of the other men. But then she gave him a smile, she lifted her pale blue-grey eyes at him and he was happy again. No, not happy exactly ; happy is the wrong word.

Drunk—that would be more like it, I imagine. Deliriously joyful on the surface; and within bottomlessly miserable. So we speculated, romantically, at long range. What we should have discovered on a nearer acquaintance I do not know—I do not want to know.

The most uninteresting human being seen at a little distance by a spectator with a lively fancy and a determination to make the most of life takes on a mysterious charm, becomes odd and exciting. One can work up a thrilling emotion about distant and unknown people—an emotion which it is impossible to recapture after personal acquaintance, but which yields place to understanding and consequent affection or antipathy.

Certain authors have exploited, either deliberately or because they could not do otherwise, their spectator's emotion in the presence of unknown actors. There is Joseph Conrad, for example. The mysterious thrilling charm of his characters, particularly his female characters, is due to the fact that he knows nothing at all about them. He sits at a distance, he watches them acting and then wonders and wonders, through pages of Marlow's winding narratives, why on earth they acted as they did, what were their motives, what they felt and thought. The God's-eye view of

32

those novelists who really know, or pretend they know, exactly what is going on in the minds of their characters, is exchanged for the traveller's-eye view, the view of the stranger who starts with no knowledge whatever of the actors' personalities and can only infer from their gestures what is happening in their minds. Conrad, it must be admitted, manages to infer very little ; he lacks the palaeontologist's imagination, has little power of reconstructing thought from seen behaviour At the end of a novel, his heroines are as shadowy as they were at the beginning. They have acted, and Conrad has lengthily wondered—without discovering—why they have acted in this particular way. His bewilderment is infectious ; the reader is just as hopelessly puzzled as the author and, incidentally, finds the characters just as wonderfully mysterious. Mystery is delightful and exciting ; but it is foolish to admire it too highly. A thing is mysterious merely because it is unknown. There will always be mysteries because there will always be unknown and unknowable things. But it is best to know what is knowable. There is no credit about not knowing what can be known. Some literary men, for example, positively pride themselves on their ignorance of science ; they are fools and arrogant

c   33

at that. If Conrad's characters are mysterious, it is not because they are complicated, difficult or subtle characters, but simply because he does not understand them ; not knowing what they are like, he speculates, unsuccessfully, and finally admits that he finds them inscrutable. The honesty with which he confesses his ignorance is meritorious, not the ignorance. The characters of the great novelists, like Dostoievsky and Tolstoy, are not mysterious ; they are perfectly well understood and clearly displayed. Such writers live with their creations. Conrad only looks on from a distance, without understanding them, without even making up plausible hypotheses about them out of his imagination.

He differs in this respect from Miss Katherine Mansfield, another writer who takes the traveller's-eye view of human beings. For Miss Mansfield has a lively fancy. Like Conrad, she sees her characters from a distance, as though at another table in a café : she overhears snatches of their conversations—about their aunts in Battersea, their stamp collections, their souls—and she finds them extraordinary, charming beyond all real and knowable people, odd, immensely exciting. She finds that they are Life itself— lovely, fantastic Life. Very rarely does she go

34

beyond this long-range café acquaintanceship with her personages, rarely makes herself at home in their flat everyday lives. But where Conrad bewilderedly speculates, Miss Mansfield uses her imagination. She invents suitable lives for the fabulous creatures glimpsed at the café. And how thrilling those fancied lives always are ! Thrilling, but just for that reason not very convincing. Miss Mansfield's studies of interiors are like those brilliant palaeontological reconstructions one sees in books of popular science—the ichthyosaurus in its native waters, pterodactyls fluttering and swooping in the tepid tertiary sky—too excitingly romantic, in spite of their air of realism, to be quite genuine. Her characters are seen with an extraordinary brilliance and precision, as one sees a party of people in a lighted drawing-room, at night, through an uncurtained window—one of those mysteriously significant Parties in Parlours of which we read in *Peter Bell* :

> Some sipping punch, some sipping tea,
> And all as silent as could be,
> All silent, and all damned.

One sees them for a moment, haloed with significance. They seem fabulous (though of course, in point of actual fact and to those sitting in the room

35

with them, they are nothing of the kind). Then one passes, they disappear. Each of Miss Mansfield's stories is a window into a lighted room. The glimpse of the inhabitants sipping their tea and punch is enormously exciting. But one knows nothing, when one has passed, of what they are really like. That is why, however thrilling at a first reading, her stories do not wear. Tchekov's do ; but then he had lived with his people as well as looked at them through the window. The traveller's-eye view of men and women is not satisfying. A man might spend his life in trains and restaurants and know nothing of humanity at the end. To know, one must be an actor as well as a spectator. One must dine at home as well as in restaurants, must give up the amusing game of peeping in at unknown windows to live quietly, flatly, unexcitingly indoors. Still, the game, if it is kept as an occasional diversion and not treated as the serious business of life, is a very good one. And on a journey it is your only travelling picquet.

GUIDE-BOOKS

FOR every traveller who has any taste of his own, the only useful guide-book will be the one which he himself has written. All others are an exasperation. They mark with asterisks the works of art which he finds dull, and they pass over in silence those which he admires. They make him travel long miles to see a mound of rubbish ; they go into ecstasies over mere antiquity. Their practical information is invariably out of date. They recommend bad hotels and qualify good ones as 'modest.' In a word, they are intolerable.

How often I have cursed Baron Baedeker for sending me through the dust to see some nauseating Sodoma or drearily respectable Andrea del Sarto ! How angry I have been with him for starring what is old merely because it is old ! And how I have hated him for his lack of discrimination ! He has a way of lumping all old things of one class together and treating them as if, being made at the same period, their merit were exactly equal. For example, the stained glass windows at Sens are treated by the guide-books as though they were just like all other stained glass of the fourteenth century, when in fact they are unique in boldness and beauty of design. Some very great artist made the series of Bible illustrations at Sens.   The Baron speaks as highly of the competent craftsman's work at Chartres and Canterbury.

Similarly the monuments in the church of Brou and the choir screen at Chartres get as many stars as the tomb of Ilaria del Carretto at Lucca, or Della Robbia's bas-relief in the Opera del Duomo at Florence. They are all of them specimens of Renaissance sculpture. There is only this slight difference between them : that the Italian works happen to be consummate masterpieces, while the French are mere barbarisms—that at Brou positively and piercingly vulgar, that at Chartres well-meaning, laborious, and sincerely dull.   And so totally does the Baron lack a sense of proportion that he gives as many stars to the church of Brou as to Bourges cathedral, recommending with equal enthusiasm a horrible little architectural nightmare and the grandest, the most strangely and fabulously beautiful building in Europe.

Imbecile ! But a learned, and, alas, indispensable imbecile. There is no escape ; one must travel in his company—at any rate on a first journey. It is only after having scrupulously done what Baedeker commands, after having discovered the Baron's lapses in taste, his artistic prejudices and antiquarian snobberies, that the tourist can compile that personal guide which is the only guide for him. If he had but possessed it on his first tour! But alas, though it is easy to take other people in by your picturesque accounts of places you have never seen, it is hard to take in yourself. The personal guide-book must be the fruit of bitter personal experience.

The only satisfactory substitute for a guide written by oneself is a guide which is copiously illustrated. To know the images of things is the next best to knowing the things themselves. Illustrations allow one to see what precisely it is that the Baron is recommending. A reproduction of those luscious Sodomas would enable one to discount the asterisks in the text. A few photographs of the tombs at Tarquinia would convince one that they were incomparably better worth looking at than the Forum. A picture of the church of Brou would excuse one from ever going near it. The best illustrated guide I know is Pampaloni's Road Book of Tuscany, in which the usual information is briefly summarized, the main routes from place to place described and nothing starred that is not reproduced in a photograph.

For some tastes, I know, Pampaloni seems a little too dry. All the cackle—even as much of it as gets into Baedeker—is cut, and one is left only with a telegraphic statement of facts and the photographs. Personally I have no great weakness for cackle (unless it be the cackle of genius) and so find Pampaloni perfectly satisfying. Many tourists, however, prefer a more literary guide. They like sentiment, and purple passages and states of soul in front of the Colosseum by moonlight, and all the rest. So do I—but not from the pens of the sort of people who write chatty guides. To me, even Baedeker seems at times rather too lyrical. I like my guides to be informative, unenthusiastic and, where practical matters are concerned, up-to-date—which Baedeker, by the way (reluctant, I suppose, for patriotic reasons to acknowledge the fact of the late War) is not. If I want cackle I take with me a better stylist than the Baron or his gushing substitutes.

The only literary guides I enjoy are the really bad ones—so bad that their badness makes, so to speak, a full circle and becomes something sublime. Your ordinary literary guides are never bad in this superlative way. Theirs is that well-

bred, efficient mediocrity for which there is
nothing whatever to be said. It is only in obscure
local guides that one finds the sublimely ludicrous.
In any town it is always worth taking a look at the
local guide. If you are lucky you will find one
in which a train is called 'Stephenson's magic
babe.' Not often, I admit (for it is not every day
that a genius is born who can hit on such felici-
ties) ; but often enough to make the search worth
while. I myself have found some notable passages in local Italian guides. This description
of a sixth-rate 'Venus rising from the Sea' is
juicy : '*Venere, abbigliata di una calda nudità,
sorge dalle onde.* . . . *È una seducente figura di
donna, palpitante, voluttuosa. Sembra che sotto
l'epidermide pulsino le vene frementi e scorre tepido
il sangue. L'occhio languido pare inviti a una
dolce tregenda.*' D'Annunzio himself could hardly
have done better. But the finest specimen of
the guide-book style I have ever met with was in
France. It is a description of Dijon. '*Comme
une jolie femme dont une maturité savoureuse
arrondit les formes plus pleines, la capitale de la
Bourgogne a fait, en grandissant, éclater la tunique
étroite de ses vieilles murailles ; elle a revêtu la robe
plus moderne et plus confortable des larges boule-
vards, des places spacieuses, des faubourgs s'égrenant*

dans les jardins ; mais elle a gardé le corps aux lignes pures, aux charmants détails que des siècles épris d'art avaient amoureusement orné.' Hats off to France ! It is with alacrity, on this occasion, that I accede to Lord Rothermere's request.

Old guide-books, so out of date as to be historical documents, make excellent travelling-companions. An early Murray is a treasure. Indeed, any volume of European travels, however dull, is interesting, provided that it be written before the age of railways and Ruskin. It is delightful to read on the spot the impressions and opinions of tourists who visited a hundred years ago, in the vehicles and with the aesthetic prejudices of the period, the places which you are visiting now. The voyage ceases to be a mere tour through space ; you travel through time and thought as well. They are morally wholesome reading too, these old books of travel ; for they make one realize the entirely accidental character of all our tastes and our fundamental intellectual beliefs. It seems to us axiomatic, for example, that Giotto was a great artist ; and yet Goethe, when he went to Assisi, did not even take the trouble to look at the frescoes in the church. For him, the only thing worth seeing at Assisi was the portico of the Roman temple. We for our part cannot get much pleasure out of Guercino ; and yet Stendhal was ravished by him. We find Canova 'amusing' and sometimes, as in the statue of Pauline Borghese, really charming in a soft, voluptuous way (the very cushion on which she reclines bulges out voluptuously ; one is reminded of those positively indecent clouds over which Correggio's angels look down at one from the dome at Parma). But we cannot quite agree with Byron when he says 'Such as the Great of yore, Canova is to-day.' And yet after all, Goethe, Stendhal, and Byron were no fools. Given their upbringing, they could not have thought differently. We would have thought just as they did, if we had lived a hundred years ago. Our altered standards of appreciation and generally greater tolerance are chiefly the result of increased acquaintance with the art of every nation and period—an acquaintance due in its turn chiefly to photography. The vastly greater part of the world's art has been non-realistic ; we know the world's art as our ancestors never did ; it is therefore only to be expected that we should be much more favourably disposed to non-realistic art, much less impressed by realism as such than men who were brought up almost exclusively in the knowledge of Greek, Roman and modern realism. These old books teach us not to be too arrogant and cocksure in our judgments. We too shall look foolish in our turn.

There are so many of these old books and they are all so characteristic of their epoch, that one can select them almost at random from the shelves of a well-stocked library, certain that whatever one lights on will be entertaining and instructive reading. Speaking from my own personal experience, I have always found Stendhal particularly agreeable as an Italian companion. The *Promenades dans Rome* have accompanied me on many of my walks in that city and never failed to please. Very enjoyable too, when one is in Rome, is the too much neglected Veuillot. I will not pretend that Veuillot is a great writer. Indeed, much of his charm and apparent originality consists in the merely accidental fact that his prejudices were unlike those which most travellers bring with them to Italy. We are so much accustomed to hearing that the temporal power was an unmixed evil and that the priests were the cause of Italy's degradation, that a man who tells us the contrary seems startlingly original. After the denunciations of so many Protestants and free-thinkers we read his book, if it be tolerably well

44

written (and Veuillot was a first-rate journalist), with a special pleasure. (It is, in the same way, the unusualness of the point of view from which it is written that makes *Les Paysans* of Balzac seem an even more remarkable book than it really is. We are used to reading novels in which the humble virtues of the peasant are exalted, his hard lot deplored and the tyranny of the landlord denounced. Balzac starts with the assumption that the peasant is an unmitigated ruffian and demands our sympathy for the unhappy landlord, who is represented as suffering incessant and unmerited persecution at the hands of the peasants. Balzac's reading of social history may not be correct ; but it is at least refreshingly unlike that of most novelists who deal with similar themes.) *Les Parfums de Rome* shares with *Les Paysans* the merit of being written from an unexpected point of view. Veuillot tours the papal states determined to see in them the earthly paradise. And he succeeds. His Holiness has only happy subjects. Outside this blessed fold prowl the wild beasts, Cavour, Mazzini, Garibaldi and the rest ; it is the duty of every right-thinking man to see that they do not break in. This is his theme and he finds in everything he sees excuses for recurring to it. *Les Parfums de Rome* is written

with a refreshing intemperance of language.
Veuillot, like Zimmi, was

> So over violent or over civil,
> That every man with him was God or Devil.

Moreover he was logical and had the courage of
his convictions. How admirable, for example,
is his denunciation of all pagan art on the ground
that it is not Christian ! While all the rest of
the world grovel before the Greeks and Romans,
Veuillot, the logical ultramontanist, condemns
them and all their works, on principle, con-
temptuously. It is delightful.

Of the other old travelling-companions who
have given me pleasure by the way I can only
mention a few. There is that mine of information, the Président des Brosses. No one is a
better companion on the Italian tour. Our own
Young is nearly as good in France. Miss
Berry's journals of travel are full of interest.
There are good things to be got from Lady Mary
Montagu. Beckford is the perfect dilettante.
But plain Bible-selling Borrow has the credit of
being the first man to appreciate El Greco.

If pictures are not your chief interest, there is
the admirable Dr. Burney, whose *Musical Tours*
are as instructive as they are delightful. His

Italian volumes are valuable, among many other reasons, because they make one realize what had happened, during the eighteenth century, to all the prodigious talent which had gone, in the past, to painting pictures, carving statues and building churches. It had all gone into music. The very street players were accomplished contrapuntists ; the peasants sang divinely (you should hear the way they sing now !), every church had a good choir which was perpetually producing new masses, motets and oratorios ; there was hardly a lady or gentleman who was not a first-rate amateur performer ; there were innumerable concerts. Dr. Burney found it a musician's paradise. And what has happened to Italian genius nowadays ? Does it still exist ? or is it dead ?

It still exists, I think ; but it has been deflected out of music, as it was deflected out of the visual arts, into politics and, later, into business and engineering. The first two-thirds of the nineteenth century were sufficiently occupied in the achievement of freedom and unity. The sixty years since then have been devoted to the exploitation of the country's resources ; and such energy as has been left over from that task has gone into politics. One day, when they have finished putting modern comfort into the old house, have turned out the obstreperous servants and installed a quiet, honest housekeeper—one day, perhaps, the Italians will allow their energy and their talent to flow back into the old channels. Let us hope they will.

SPECTACLES

I NEVER move without a plentiful supply of optical glass. A pair of spectacles for reading, a pair for long range, with a couple of monocles in reserve—these go with me everywhere. To break all these, it would need an earthquake or a railway accident. And absence of mind would have to be carried to idiocy before they could all be lost. Moreover, there is a further safety in a numerous supply : for matter, who can doubt it ? is not neutral, as the men of science falsely teach, but slightly malignant, on the side of the devils against us. This being so, one pair of spectacles must inevitably break or lose itself, just when you can least afford to do without and are least able to replace it. But inanimate matter, so called, is no fool ; and when a pair of spectacles realizes that you carry two or three other pairs in your pockets and suit-cases, it will understand that the game is hopeless and, so far from deliberately smashing or losing itself, will take pains to remain intact.

But when, in any month after the vernal equinox and before the autumn, my wanderings take me southwards, towards the sun, my armoury of spectacles is enlarged by the addition of three pairs of coloured glasses—two of lighter and darker shades of green, and one black. The glare from dusty roads, from white walls and the metallic, blue-hot sky is painful and even dangerous. As the summer advances or retreats, as the light of each day waxes or declines, I adjust to my nose the pale green, the dark green or the black spectacles. In this way I am able to temper the illumination of the world to my exact requirements.

But even if I suffered not at all from excess of light and could perform without winking the feats of the eagle and the oxy-acetylene welder, I should still take coloured glasses with me on my southward travels. For they have an aesthetic as well as a merely practical use. They improve the landscape as well as soothe the eyes.

As one approaches the great desert belt which bands the earth with some thousand miles of aridity to this side of the tropic of Cancer, the landscape suffers a change which to us northerners at least seems a change for the worse. It loses its luxuriant greenness. South of Lyons (except among the mountains and in the marshes) there is no grass worthy of the name. The deciduous trees grow with reluctance, yielding place to the black cypress and pine, the dark green laurel and juniper, the pale grey olive. The greens in an Italian landscape are either pale and dusty or glossily dark. Only when you climb to two thousand feet—and by no means invariably then—does anything like the brilliant, the seemingly self-luminous verdure of the English scene appear. The typical north Italian landscape is one of hills, the lower slopes grey with olives, the summits, when they are above the level of cultivation, bare and brown. It is a landscape that makes a not entirely satisfactory compromise between the northern type and the fully southern. The English scene is made rich and comfortable by the bosomy forms and the damply glowing colours of its luxuriant foliage. And its rather rotund earthiness is tempered and made romantic by the bloom of mist that half veils it from sight. The southern, Mediterranean landscape, which makes its first Italian appearance at Terracina, is bare, sharp-outlined and austerely brilliant. The air is clear, and the far-seen earth seems itself to be made of coloured air. The landscape of Northern Italy is neither northern nor southern —neither aerially bright and light nor, on the other hand, rounded, or softly, luxuriously green.

It is here, in this half-parched landscape that is not yet refined to a bright asceticism, that the judicious traveller will don his green spectacles.

The effect is magical. Every blade of dusty grass becomes on the instant rich with juicy life. Whatever greenness lurks in the grey of the olive trees shines out, intensified. The dried-up woods reburgeon. The vines and the growing corn seem to have drunk of a refreshing rain. All that the scene lacked to make it perfectly beautiful is instantaneously added. Through green spectacles, it becomes the northern landscape, but transformed and glorified—brighter, more nobly dramatic and romantic.

Green spectacles make excellent wearing, too, on the shores of the northern Mediterranean. In the south the blue of the sea is beautifully dark, like lapis-lazuli. It is the wine-dark sea of antiquity in contrast with which the sunlit land seems more than ever light, clear-coloured and aerial. But north of Rome the blue is insufficiently intense ; it is a china not a lazuline blue. The sea at Monaco and Genoa, at Spezia and Civitavecchia has the blue, glassy stare of a doll's eye—a stare that becomes very soon enraging in its enormous blankness and brightness. Put on green spectacles and this blank stare becomes at once the darkly glaucous, enigmatic gaze that shines up, between the cypresses, from the pools in the Villa d'Este gardens at Tivoli. From imbecile, the sea turns siren, and the arid hills that overhang it break into verdure as though beneath the feet of the spring.

Or if you like, you may put on black spectacles and so deepen the colour till it approaches that of the wine-dark Mediterranean of Greece and Magna Graecia and the isles. Black spectacles do nothing, however, to make the land more southern in aspect. By the side of their dark sea, the southern coasts seem built of bright air. Black spectacles may darken the northern sea; but they also give weight and an added solidity to the land. The glass which shall make the world seem brighter, clearer and lighter, put sunlight into the grey landscape and turn north into south still, alas, remains to be invented.

I⊤ is a curious fact, of which I can think of no satisfactory explanation, that enthusiasm for country life and love of natural scenery are strongest and most widely diffused precisely in those European countries which have the worst climate and where the search for the picturesque involves the greatest discomfort. Nature worship increases in an exact ratio with distance from the Mediterranean. The Italians and the Spanish have next to no interest in nature for its own sake. The French feel a certain affection for the country, but not enough to make them desire to live in it if they can possibly inhabit the town. The south Germans and Swiss form an apparent exception to the rule. They live nearer to the Mediterranean than the Parisians, and yet they are fonder of the country. But the exception, as I have said, is only apparent; for owing to their remoteness from the ocean and the mountainous conformation of the land, these people enjoy for a large part of each year a climate that is, to all intents, arctic. In England, where the climate is detestable, we love the country so much that we are prepared, for the privilege of living in it, to get up at seven, summer and winter, bicycle, wet or fine, to a distant station and make an hour's journey to our place of labour. In our spare moments we go for walking tours, and we regard caravanning as a pleasure. In Holland the climate is far more unpleasant than in England and we should consequently expect the Dutch to be even keener country-fanciers than ourselves. The ubiquitous water makes it difficult, however, for season-ticket holders to settle down casually in the Dutch countryside. But if unsuitable as building land, the soggy meadows of the Low Countries are firm enough to carry tents. Unable to live permanently in the country, the Dutch are the greatest campers in the world. Poor Uncle Toby, when he was campaigning in those parts, found the damp so penetrating, that he was forced to burn good brandy in his tent to dry the air. But then my Uncle Toby was a mere Englishman, brought up in a climate which, compared with that of Holland, is balmy. The hardier Dutch camp out for pleasure. Of Northern Germany it is enough to say that it is the home of the wander-birds. And as for Scandinavia—it is well known that there is no part of the world, excluding the tropics, where people so freely divest themselves of their clothing. The Swedish passion for nature is so strong that it can

only be adequately expressed when in a state of
nature. 'As souls unbodied,' says Donne,
'bodies unclothed must be to taste whole joys.'
Noble, nude and far more modern than any other
people in Europe, they sport in the icy waters of
the Baltic, they roam naked in the primeval
forest. The cautious Italian, meanwhile, bathes
in his tepid sea during only two months out of the
twelve ; always wears a vest under his shirt and
never leaves the town, if he can possibly help it,
except when the summer is at its most hellish, and
again, for a little while, in the autumn, to super-
intend the making of his wine.

Strange and inexplicable state of affairs ! Is
it that the dwellers under inclement skies are
trying to bluff themselves into a belief that they
inhabit Eden ? Do they deliberately love nature
in the hope of persuading themselves that she is
as beautiful in the damp and darkness as in the
sunlight ? Do they brave the discomforts of
northern country life in order to be able to say to
those who live in more favoured lands : You see,
our countryside is just as delightful as yours ;
and the proof is that we live in it !

But whatever the reason, the fact remains that
nature worship does increase with distance from
the sun. To search for causes is hopeless ; but

it is easy and at the same time not uninteresting
to catalogue effects. Thus, our Anglo-Saxon
passion for the country has had the result of turning the country into one vast town ; but a town
without the urban conveniences which makes
tolerable life in a city. For we all love the
country so much, that we desire to live in it, if
only during the night, when we are not at work.
We build cottages, buy season tickets and bicycles
to take us to the station. And meanwhile the
country perishes. The Surrey I knew as a boy
was full of wildernesses. To-day Hindhead is
hardly distinguishable from the Elephant and
Castle. Mr. Lloyd George has built a week-end
cottage (not, one feels, without a certain apposite-
ness) at the foot of the Devil's Jumps ; and
several thousand people are busily following his
example. Every lane is now a street. Harrod's
and Selfridge's call daily. There is no more
country, at any rate within fifty miles of London.
Our love has killed it.

Except in summer, when it is too hot to stay
in town, the French, and still more, the Italians,
do not like the country. The result is that they
still have country not to like. Solitude stretches
almost to the gates of Paris. (And Paris, remember, still has gates ; you drive up to them

along country roads, enter and find yourself
within a few minutes of the centre of the city).
The silence sleeps unbroken, except by the faint
music of ghosts, within a mile of the Victor
Emanuel monument at Rome.

In France, in Italy none but countrymen live
in the country. Agriculture there is taken seriously ; farms are still farms and not week-end
cottages ; and the corn is still permitted to grow
on what, in England, would be desirable building
land.

In Italy, despite the fact that the educated
Italians like the country still less than the French,
there are fewer complete solitudes than in France,
because there are more countrymen. And how
few there are in France ! A drive from the
Belgian frontier to the Mediterranean puts life
and meaning into those statistics from which we
learn, academically and in theory, that France is
under-populated. Long stretches of open road
extend between town and town.

> Like stones of worth they thinly placed are,
> Or captain jewels in the carcanet.

Even the villages are few and far between. And
those innumerable farms which shine out from
among the olive trees on Italian hill-sides—one

looks in vain for their French counterpart. Driving through the fertile plains of Central France, one can turn one's eyes over the fields and scarcely see a house. And then, what forests still grown on French soil ! Huge tracts of uninhabited woodland, with not a week-ender or a walking-tourist to be seen within their shades.

This state of things is delightful to me personally ; for I like the country, enjoy solitude, and take no interest in the political future of France. But to a French patriot I can imagine that a drive across his native land must seem depressing. Huge populations, upon whose skulls the bump of philoprogenitiveness can be seen at a quarter of a mile, pullulate on the further side of almost every frontier. Without haste, without rest, as though by a steadily continued miracle, the Germans and the Italians multiply themselves, like loaves and fishes. Every three years a million brand new Teutons peer across the Rhine, a million Italians are wondering where they are going to find room, in their narrow country, to live. And there are no more Frenchmen. Twenty years hence, what will happen ? The French Government offers prizes to those who produce large families. In vain ; everybody knows all about birth control and even in the least educated classes there are no prejudices and a great deal of thrift. Hordes of blackamoors are drilled and armed ; but blackamoors can be but a poor defence, in the long run, against European philoprogenitiveness. Sooner or later, this half-empty land will be colonized. It may be done peacefully, it may be done with violence ; let us hope peacefully, with the consent and at the invitation of the French themselves. Already the French import, temporarily, I forget how many foreign labourers every year. In time, no doubt, the foreigners will begin to settle : the Italians in the south, the Germans in the east, the Belgians in the north, perhaps even a few English in the west.

Frenchmen may not like the plan ; but until all nations agree to practise birth control to exactly the same extent, it is the best that can be devised.

The Portuguese who, in the later sixteenth and the seventeenth century, suffered acutely from under-population (half the able-bodied men had emigrated to the colonies, where they died in war or of tropical diseases, while those who stayed at home were periodically decimated by famine— for the colonies produced only gold, not bread) solved their problem by importing negro slaves to work the deserted fields. The negroes settled. They intermarried with the inhabitants. In two or three generations the race which had conquered half the world was extinct, and Portugal, with the exception of a small area in the north, was inhabited by a hybrid race of Eur-Africans. The French may think themselves lucky if, avoiding war, they can fill their depleted country with civilized white men.

Meanwhile, the emptiness of France is a delight to every lover of nature and solitude. But even in Italy, where farms and peasants and peasants' children are thick on the land, the lover of the country feels much happier than he does in what may actually be more sparsely inhabited districts of the home counties. For farms and peasants are country products, as truly native to the land as trees or growing corn, and as inoffensive. It is the urban interloper who ruins the English country. Neither he nor his house belong to it. In Italy, on the other hand, when the rare trespasser from the town does venture into the country, he finds it genuinely rustic. The country is densely populated, but it is still the country. It has not been killed by the deadly kindness of those who, like myself, are nature's townsmen.

The time is not far distant, I am afraid, when every countryside in Europe, even the Spanish, will be invaded by nature lovers from the towns. It is not so long ago, after all, since Evelyn was horrified and disgusted by the spectacle of the rocks at Clifton. Till the end of the eighteenth century every sensible man, even in England, even in Sweden, feared and detested mountains. The modern enthusiasm for wild nature is a recent growth and began—along with kindness to animals, industrialism and railway travelling—among the English. (It is, perhaps, not surprising that the people which first made their cities uninhabitable with dirt, noise and smoke should also have been the first to love nature.) From this island country sentiment has spread with machinery. All the world welcomed machinery with delight ; but country sentiment has so far flourished only in the north. Still, there are evident signs that even the Latins are becoming infected by it. In France and Italy wild nature has become—though to a far less extent than in England—the object of *snobisme*. It is rather chic, in those countries, to be fond of nature. In a few years, I repeat, everybody will adore it as a matter of course. For even in the north those who do not in the least like the country are made to imagine that they do by the artful and never-ceasing suggestions of the people whose interest it is that the country should be liked. No modern man, even if he loathed the country, could resist the appeal of the innumerable adver-tisements, published by railways, motor car manu-facturers, thermos flask makers, sporting tailors, house agents and all the rest whose livelihood depends on his frequently visiting the country. Now the art of advertising in the Latin countries is still poorly developed. But it is improving even there. The march of progress is irresistible. Fiat and the State Railways have only to hire American advertising managers to turn the Italians into a race of week-enders and season-ticket holders. Already there is a *Città Giardino* on the outskirts of Rome ; Ostia is being devel-oped as a residential seaside suburb ; the recently opened motor road has placed the Lakes at the mercy of Milan. My grandchildren, I foresee, will have to take their holidays in Central Asia.

Aʟʟ tourists cherish an illusion, of which no amount of experience can ever completely cure them ; they imagine that they will find time, in the course of their travels, to do a lot of reading. They see themselves, at the end of a day's sight-seeing or motoring, or while they are sitting in the train, studiously turning over the pages of all the vast and serious works which, at ordinary seasons, they never find time to read. They start for a fortnight's tour in France, taking with them *The Critique of Pure Reason, Appearance and Reality*, the complete works of Dante and the *Golden Bough*. They come home to make the discovery that they have read something less than half a chapter of the *Golden Bough* and the first fifty-two lines of the *Inferno*. But that does not prevent them from taking just as many books the next time they set out on their travels.

Long experience has taught me to reduce in some slight measure the dimensions of my travelling library. But even now I am far too optimistic about my powers of reading while on a journey. Along with the books which I know it is possible to read, I still continue to put in a few impossible volumes in the pious hope that

some day, somehow, they will get read. Thick
tomes have travelled with me for thousands of
kilometres across the face of Europe and have
returned with their secrets unviolated. But
whereas in the past I took nothing but thick
tomes, and a great quantity of them at that, I
now take only one or two and for the rest pack
only the sort of books which I know by experience
can be read in a hotel bedroom after a day's sight-
seeing.

The qualities essential in a good travelling-
book are these. It should be a work of such a
kind that one can open it anywhere and be sure
of finding something interesting, complete in itself and susceptible of being read in a short time.
A book requiring continuous attention and prolonged mental effort is useless on a voyage ; for
leisure, when one travels, is brief and tinged with
physical fatigue, the mind distracted and unapt
to make protracted exertions.

Few travelling-books are better than a good
anthology of poetry in which every page contains
something complete and perfect in itself. The
brief respites from labour which the self-immol-
ated tourist allows himself cannot be more
delightfully filled than with the reading of poetry,
which may even be got by heart ; for the mind,

though reluctant to follow an argument, takes pleasure in the slight labour of committing melodious words to memory.

In the choice of anthologies every traveller must please himself. My own favourite is Edward Thomas's *Pocket Book of Poems and Songs for the Open Air*. Thomas was a man of wide reading and of exquisite taste, and peculiarly gifted, moreover, to be an anthologist of the Open Air. For out of the huge tribe of modern versifiers who have babbled of green fields, Thomas is almost the only one whom one feels to be a 'nature poet' (the expression is somehow rather horrible, but there is no other) by right of birth and the conquest of real sympathy and understanding. It is not every one who says Lord, Lord, that shall enter into the kingdom of heaven; and few, very few of those who cry Cuckoo, Cuckoo, shall be admitted into the company of nature poets. For proof of this I refer my readers to the various volumes of Georgian Poetry.

Equally well adapted, with poetry, to the traveller's need, are collections of aphorisms or maxims. If they are good—and they must be very good indeed ; for there is nothing more dismal than a ' Great Thought ' enunciated by an

author who has not himself the elements of greatness—maxims make the best of all reading. They
take a minute to read and provide matter upon
which thought can ruminate for hours. None
are to be preferred to La Rochefoucauld's. Myself, I always reserve my upper left-hand waist-
coat pocket for a small sexto-decimo reprint of
the *Maximes*. It is a book to which there is no
bottom or end. For with every month that one
lives, with every accession to one's knowledge,
both of oneself and of others, it means something
more. For La Rochefoucauld knew almost
everything about the human soul, so that practically every discovery one can make oneself, as
one advances through life, has been anticipated
by him and formulated in the briefest and most
elegant phrases. I say advisedly that La Rochefoucauld knew 'almost' everything about the
human soul; for it is obvious that he did not
know all. He knew everything about the souls
of human beings in so far as they are social animals.
Of the soul of man in solitude—of man when he
is no more interested in the social pleasures and
successes which were, to La Rochefoucauld, so
all-important—he knows little or nothing. If
we desire to know something about the human
soul in solitude—in its relations, not to man, but

to God—we must go elsewhere : to the Gospels, to the novels of Dostoievsky, for example. But man in his social relationships has never been more accurately described, and his motives never more delicately analysed than by La Rochefoucauld. The aphorisms vary considerably in value ; but the best of them—and their number is surprisingly large—are astonishingly profound and pregnant. They resume a vast experience. In a sentence La Rochefoucauld compresses as much material as would serve a novelist for a long story. Conversely, it would not surprise me to learn that many novelists turn to the *Maximes* for suggestions for plots and characters It is impossible, for example, to read Proust without being reminded of the *Maximes*, or the *Maximes* without being reminded of Proust. ' Le plaisir de l'amour est d'aimer, et l'on est plus heureux par la passion que l'on a que par celle que l'on donne.' ' Il y a des gens si remplis d'eux-mêmes, que, lorsqu'ils sont amoureux, ils trouvent moyen d'être occupés de leur passion sans l'être de la personne qu'ils aiment.' What are all the love stories in *A la Recherche du Temps Perdu* but enormous amplifications of these aphorisms ? Proust is La Rochefoucauld magnified ten thousand times.

Hardly less satisfactory as travel books are the

aphoristic works of Nietzsche. Nietzsche's say-
ings have this in common with La Rochefoucauld's, that they are pregnant and expansive.
His best aphorisms are long trains of thought,
compressed. The mind can dwell on them at
length because so much is implicit in them. It
is in this way that good aphorisms differ from
mere epigrams, in which the whole point consists
in the felicity of expression. An epigram pleases
by surprising ; after the first moment the effect
wears off and we are no further interested in it.
One is not taken in twice by the same practical
joke. But an aphorism does not depend on
verbal wit. Its effect is not momentary, and the
more we think of it, the more substance we find
in it.

Another excellent book for a journey—for it
combines expansive aphorisms with anecdotes—
is Boswell's *Life of Johnson*, which the Oxford
Press now issues, on India paper, in a single small
octavo volume. (All travellers, by the way, owe
much to the exertions of Henry Frowde, of the
Oxford Press, the inventor, or at least the European reinventor, of that fine rag paper, impreg-
nated with mineral matter to give it opacity,
which we call India paper.) What the aphorism
is to the philosophical treatise, the India paper

volume is to the ponderous editions of the past. All Shakespeare, perfectly legible, gets into a volume no bigger than a single novel by the late Charles Garvice. All Pepys, or as much of him as the British public is allowed to read, can now be fitted into three pockets. And the Bible, reduced to an inch in thickness, must surely be in danger of losing those bullet-stopping qualities which it used, at any rate in romantic novels, to possess. Thanks to Henry Frowde one can get a million words of reading matter into a rucksack and hardly feel the difference in its weight.

India paper and photography have rendered possible the inclusion in a portable library of what in my opinion is the best traveller's book of all— a volume (any one of the thirty-two will do) of the twelfth, half-size edition of the *Encyclopaedia Britannica*. It takes up very little room (eight and a half inches by six and a half by one is not excessive), it contains about a thousand pages and an almost countless number of curious and improbable facts. It can be dipped into anywhere, its component chapters are complete in themselves and not too long. For the traveller, disposing as he does only of brief half-hours, it is the perfect book, the more so, since I take it that, being a born traveller, he is likely also to be one of those desultory and self-indulgent readers to whom the *Encyclopaedia*, when not used for some practical purpose, must specially appeal. I never pass a day away from home without taking a volume with me. It is the book of books. Turning over its pages, rummaging among the stores of fantastically varied facts which the hazards of alphabetical arrangement bring together, I wallow in my mental vice. A stray volume of the *Encyclopaedia* is like the mind of a learned madman—stored with correct ideas, between which, however, there is no other connection than the fact that there is a B in both ; from orach, or mountain spinach, one passes directly to oracles. That one does not oneself go mad, or become, in the process of reading the *Encyclopaedia*, a mine of useless and unrelated knowledge is due to the fact that one forgets. The mind has a vast capacity for oblivion. Providentially ; otherwise, in the chaos of futile memories, it would be impossible to remember anything useful or coherent. In practice, we work with generalizations, abstracted out of the turmoil of realities. If we remembered everything perfectly, we should never be able to generalize at all ; for there would appear before our minds nothing but individual images, precise and different. Without ignorance we could not generalize. Let us thank Heaven for our powers of forgetting. With regard to the *Encyclopaedia*, they are enormous. The mind only remembers that of which it has some need. Five minutes after reading about mountain spinach, the ordinary man, who is neither a botanist nor a cook, has forgotten all about it. Read for amusement, the *Encyclopaedia* serves only to distract for the moment ; it does not instruct, it deposits nothing on the surface of the mind that will remain. It is a mere time-killer and momentary tickler of the mind. I use it only for amusement on my travels ; I should be ashamed to indulge so wantonly in mere curiosity at home, during seasons of serious business.

Part II
PLACES

Iт was March and the snow was melting. Half
wintry, half vernal, the mountain looked patchy,
like a mangy dog. The southward slopes were
bare ; but in every hollow, on the sunless side of
every tree, the snow still lay, white under the
blue transparent shadows.

We walked through a little pine wood ; the
afternoon sunlight breaking through the dark
foliage lit up here a branch, there a length of
trunk, turning the ruddy bark into a kind of
golden coral. Beyond the wood the hill lay bare
to the summit. On the very crest a mass of
buildings lifted their high sunlit walls against the
pale sky, a chilly little New Jerusalem. It was
the monastery of Montesenario. We climbed
towards it, toilsomely ; for the last stage in the
pilgrim's progress from Florence to Montesenario
is uncommonly steep and the motor must be left
behind. And suddenly, as though to welcome us,
as though to encourage our efforts, the heavenly
city disgorged a troop of angels. Turning a
corner of the track we saw them coming down to
meet us, by two and two in a long file ; angels in
black cassocks with round black hats on their
heads—a seminary taking its afternoon airing

They were young boys, the eldest sixteen or seventeen, the youngest not more than ten. Flapping along in their black skirts they walked with an unnatural decorum. It was difficult to believe, when one saw the little fellows at the head of the crocodile, with the tall Father in charge striding along at their side, it was difficult to believe that they were not masquerading. It seemed a piece of irreverent fun ; a caricature by Goya come to life. But their faces were serious ; chubby or adolescently thin, they wore already an unctuously clerical expression. It was no joke. Looking at those black-robed children, one wished that it had been.

We climbed on ; the little priestlings descended out of sight. And now at last we were at the gates of the heavenly city. A little paved and parapeted platform served as landing to the flight of steps that led up into the heart of the convent. In the middle of the platform stood a more than life-sized statue of some unheard-of saint. It was a comically admirable piece of eighteenth-century baroque. Carved with coarse brilliance, the creature gesticulated ecstatically, rolling its eyes to heaven ; its garments flapped around it in broad folds. It was not, somehow, the sort of saint one expected to see standing sentinel over the bleakest hermitage in Tuscany. And the convent itself—that too seemed incongruous on the top of this icy mountain. For the heavenly city was a handsome early baroque affair with *settecento* trimmings and additions. The church was full of twiddly gilt carvings and dreadfully competent pictures ; the remains of the seven pious Florentines who, in the thirteenth century, fled from the city of destruction in the plain below, and founded this hermitage on the mountain, were coffered in a large gold and crystal box, illuminated, like a show-case in the drawing-room of a collector of porcelain, by concealed electric lights. No, the buildings were ludicrous. But after all, what do buildings matter ? A man can paint beautiful pictures in a slum, can write poetry in Wigan ; and conversely he can live in an exquisite house, surrounded by masterpieces of ancient art and yet (as one sees almost invariably when collectors of the antique, relying for once on their own judgment, and not on tradition, ' go in for ' modern art) be crassly insensitive and utterly without taste. Within certain limits, environment counts for very little. It is only when environment is extremely unfavourable that it can blast or distort the powers of the mind. And however favourable, it can do nothing to extend the limits set by nature to a man's ability. So here the architecture seemed impossibly incongruous with the bleak place, with the very notion of a hermitage ; but the hermits who live in the midst of it are probably not even aware of its existence. In the shade of the absurd statue of San Filippo Benizi a Buddha would be able to think as Buddhistically as beneath the bo-tree.

In the grounds of the monastery we saw half a dozen black-frocked Servites sawing wood— sawing with vigour and humility, in spite of the twiddly gilding in the church and the *settecento* bell tower. They looked the genuine article. And the view from the mountain's second peak was in the grandest eremitic tradition. The hills stretched away as far as the eye could reach into the wintry haze, like a vast heaving sea frozen to stillness. The valleys were filled with blue shadow, and all the sunward slopes were the colour of rusty gold. At our feet the ground fell away into an immense blue gulf. The gauzy air softened every outline, smoothed away every detail, leaving only golden lights and violet shadows floating like the disembodied essence of a landscape, under the pale sky.

We stood for a long time looking out over that kingdom of silence and solemn beauty. The solitude was as profound as the shadowy gulf beneath us ; it stretched to the misty horizons and up into the topless sky.   Here at the heart of it, I thought, a man might begin to understand something about that part of his being which does not reveal itself in the quotidian commerce of life ; which the social contacts do not draw forth, spark-like, from the sleeping flint that is an untried spirit ; that part of him, of whose very existence he is only made aware in solitude and silence.   And if there happens to be no silence in his life, if he is never solitary, then he may go down to his grave without a knowledge of its existence, much less an understanding of its nature or realization of its potentialities.

We retraced our steps to the monastery and thence walked down the steep path to the motor. A mile further down the road towards Pratolino, we met the priestlings returning from their walk. Poor children ! But was their lot worse, I wondered, than that of the inhabitants of the city in the valley ?   On their mountain top they lived under a tyrannous rule, they were taught to believe in a number of things manifestly silly. But was the rule any more tyrannous than that of the imbecile conventions which control the lives of social beings in the plain ?   Was snobbery about duchesses and distinguished novelists more reasonable than snobbery about Jesus Christ and the Saints ?   Was hard work to the greater glory of God more detestable than eight hours a day in an office for the greater enrichment of the Jews ? Temperance was a bore, no doubt ; but was it so nauseatingly wearisome as excess ?   And the expense of spirit in prayer and meditation—was that so much less amusing than the expense of spirit in a waste of shame ?   Driving down towards the city in the plain, I wondered.   And when, in the Via Tornabuoni, we passed Mrs. Thingummy, in the act of laboriously squeezing herself out on to the pavement through the door of her gigantic limousine, I suddenly and perfectly understood what it was that had made those seven rich Florentine merchants, seven hundred years ago, abandon their position in the world, and had sent them up into the high wilderness, to live in holes at the top of Montesenario.   I looked back ; Mrs. Thingummy was waddling across the pavement into the jeweller's shop. Yes, I perfectly understood.

THE river flows in a narrow valley between
hills. A broad, a brimming and a shining river.
The hills are steep and all of a height. Where
the river bends, the hills on one side jut forward
in a bastion, the hills on the other retreat. There
are cliffs, there are hanging woods, dark with
foliage. The sky is pale above this strip of fantastically carved and scalloped earth. A pale sky
from which it must sometimes rain Chinese
white. For there is an ashen pallor over the
rocks ; and the green of the grass and the trees
is tinged with white till it has taken on the colour
of the 'Emerald Green' of children's paint-
boxes.

Brimming and shining river, pale crags, and
trees richly dark, slopes where the turf is the
colour of whitened verdigris—I took these things
for fancies. Peering into the little pictures, each
painted with a million tiny strokes of a four-
haired sable brush, I laughed with pleasure at the
beauty of the charming invention. This Joachim
Patinir, I thought, imagines delicately. For
years I was accustomed to float along that crag-
reflecting river as down a river of the mind, out
of the world.

F　　　　81

And then one day—one wet day in autumn—driving out of Namur towards Dinant through the rain, suddenly I found myself rolling, as fast as ten horses ventured to take me through the slippery mud, along the bank of this imaginary stream. The rain, it is true, a little blurred the scene. Greyly it hung, like a dirty glass, between the picture and the beholder's eye. But through it, unmistakably, I distinguished the fabulous landscape of the Fleming's little paintings. Crags, river, emerald green slopes, dark woods were there, indubitably real. I had given to Joachim Patinir the credit that was due to God. What I had taken for his exquisite invention was the real and actual Meuse.

Mile after mile we drove, from Namur to Dinant ; from Dinant, mile after mile, to Givet And it was Patinir all the way ; winding river, the double line of jutting and re-entrant hill, verdigris grass, cliffs and pensile trees all the way. At Givet we left the river ; for our destination was Reims and our road led us through Rethel. We left the river, but left it with the impression that it wound back, Patinir landscape after Patinir landscape, all the way to its distant source at Poissy. I should like to think, indeed, that it did. For Patinir was a charming painter and his surviving works are few. Two hundred miles of him would not be at all too much.

THE sky was Tiepolo's palette. A cloud of smoke mounted into the blue, white where it looked towards the sun and darkening, through the colour of the shadowed folds in a wedding gown, to grey. In the foreground on the right a tall pink house went up, glowing like a geranium, into the sunlight. There was the stuff there for a Madonna with attendant saints and angels ; or a scene from Trojan history ; or a Crucifixion ; or one of the little amours of Jupiter Tonans.

The earth was Mediterranean—a piece of the Riviera completely surrounded by water. In a word, Elba. The hills dived down into a handsomely curved bay, full of bright, staring blue sea. On the headland at one end of the bay Portoferraio was piled up in tiers of painted stucco. At its feet lay a little harbour bristling with masts A smell of fish and the memory of Napoleon haunted the atmosphere inveterately. Conscience and Baron Baedeker had told us that we ought to visit Napoleon's house—now, very suitably, a natural history museum. But we had hardened our hearts and would not go. It is very unpleasant not to have done one's duty. ' How tedious is a guilty conscience,' says the Cardinal in the *Duchess of Malfi*. He was quite right. We had walked the blazing streets groaning under conviction of sin.

And then, passing through a gateway in the walls of the old town, we found ourselves confronted by a scene that entirely relieved us of all our sense of guilt. For we were looking at something compared with which a house full of Napoleonic souvenirs was so obviously second-rate and dull that our rebellion against Baedeker ceased to be criminal and became positively meritorious.

Below us, on the further side of a blue inlet of the sea, and with the mountains behind it, lay a little piece of the Black Country. In the midst stood a group of blast furnaces with three huge chimneys rising from beside them like the bell towers of a cathedral. To the right of them were five or six more chimneys. Three huge cranes were perched at the water's edge, and an iron bridge led from the wharves inland to the furnaces. The chimneys, the cranes, the furnaces and buildings, the heap of rubbish, the very ground in this little area between the Mediterranean and the mountains—all were soot-black. Black against the sky, black against the golden-glaucous hills, blackly reflected in the shining blue water.

I should have painted the scene if I had known how. It was exceedingly beautiful. Beautiful and dramatic too. The mind delights in violent contrasts. Birmingham is frightful enough where it is, its body in Warwickshire and its sooty tentacles stretching out across the undulating land into Stafford. But set it down in Sicily or on the shores of Lago Maggiore and its frightfulness becomes at once more painfully apparent. In Warwickshire it is a full-length sermon on civilization, but one sleeps through sermons. Beside the Mediterranean it becomes the most bitingly memorable of epigrams. Moreover, the actual Birmingham of Warwickshire is too large to be taken in as a whole. This single piece of blackness between the blue sky and the blue sea was compactly symbolic. And because the sky and the grass were still visible all round it, the contest between industrialism and the natural beauties of the earth was much more vividly realized than where, as in the great towns of the north, industrialism has completely triumphed and one is not even aware of the existence of what has been conquered.

We stood for a long time, watching the smoke

from the chimneys as it mounted into the still air. White gauze ; white satin, glossy or shadowed ; feathery grey—Tiepolo's angels hovered ; and the blue sky was the Madonna's silken robe ; and the tall pink house on our right was the colour of one of those very handsome velvets to which, in the paradise of the last of the Venetians, the blest are so excusably partial.

Our rooms were in a tower. From the windows one looked across the brown tiled roofs to where, on its hill, stood the cathedral. A hundred feet below was the street, a narrow canyon between high walls, perennially sunless ; the voices of the passers-by came up, reverberating, as out of a chasm. Down there they walked always in shadow ; but in our tower we were the last to lose the sunlight   On the hot days it was cooler, no doubt, down in the street ; but we at least had the winds. The waves of the air broke against our tower and flowed past it on either side. And at evening, when only the belfries and the domes and the highest roofs were still flushed by the declining sun, our windows were level with the flight of the swifts and swallows. Sunset after sunset all through the long summer, they wheeled and darted round our tower. There was always a swarm of them intricately manœuvring just outside the window. They swerved this way and that, they dipped and rose, they checked their headlong flight with a flutter of their long pointed wings and turned about within their own length. Compact, smooth and tapering, they seemed the incarnation of airy speed.

And their thin, sharp, arrowy cry was speed made audible. I have sat at my window watching them tracing their intricate arabesques until I grew dizzy ; till their shrill crying sounded as though from within my ears and their flying seemed a motion, incessant, swift and bewilderingly multitudinous, behind my eyes. And all the while the sun declined, the shadows climbed higher up the houses and towers, and the light with which they were tipped became more rosy And at last the shadow had climbed to the very top and the city lay in a grey and violet twilight beneath the pale sky.

One evening, towards the end of June, as I was sitting at the window looking at the wheeling birds, I heard through the crying of the swifts the sound of a drum. I looked down into the shadowy street, but could see nothing. Rub-a-dub, dub, dub, dub—the sound grew louder and louder, and suddenly there appeared round the corner where our street bent out of sight, three personages out of a Pinturicchio fresco. They were dressed in liveries of green and yellow— yellow doublets slashed and tagged with green, parti-coloured hose and shoes, with feathered caps of the same colours. Their leader played the drum. The two who followed carried green and yellow banners. Immediately below our tower the street opens out a little into a tiny piazza. In this clear space the three Pinturicchio figures came to a halt and the crowd of little boys and loafers who followed at their heels grouped themselves round to watch. The drummer quickened his beat and the two banner-bearers stepped forward into the middle of the little square. They stood there for a moment quite still, the right foot a little in advance of the other, the left fist on the hip and the lowered banners drooping from the right. Then, together, they lifted the banners and began to wave them round their heads. In the wind of their motion the flags opened out. They were the same size and both of them green and yellow, but the colours were arranged in a different pattern on each. And what patterns ! Nothing more ' modern ' was ever seen. They might have been designed by Picasso for the Russian Ballet. Had they been by Picasso, the graver critics would have called them futuristic, the sprightlier (I must apologize for both these expressions) jazz. But the flags were not Picasso's ; they were designed some four hundred years ago by the nameless genius who dressed the Sienese for their yearly pageant. This being the case, the critics can only take off their hats.

The flags are classical, they are High Art; there is nothing more to be said.

The drum beat on. The bannermen waved their flags, so artfully that the whole expanse of patterned stuff was always unfurled and tremulously stretched along the air. They passed the flags from one hand to the other, behind their backs, under a lifted leg. Then, at last, drawing themselves together to make a supreme effort, they tossed their banners into the air. High they rose, turning slowly, over and over, hung for an instant at the height of their trajectory, then dropped back, the weighted stave foremost, towards their throwers, who caught them as they fell. A final wave, then the drum returned to its march rhythm, the bannermen shouldered their flags, and followed by the anachronistic children and idlers from the twentieth century, Pinturicchio's three young bravos swaggered off up the dark street out of sight and at length, the drum taps coming faintlier and ever faintlier, out of hearing.

Every evening after that, while the swallows were in full cry and flight about the tower, we heard the beating of the drum. Every evening, in the little piazza below us, a fragment of Pinturicchio came to life. Sometimes it was our friends in green and yellow who returned to wave their flags beneath our windows. Sometimes it was men from the other *contrade* or districts of the town, in blue and white, red and white, black, white and orange, white, green and red, yellow and scarlet. Their bright pied doublets and parti-coloured hose shone out from among the drabs and funereal blacks of the twentieth-century crowd that surrounded them. Their spread flags waved in the street below, like the painted wings of enormous butterflies. The drummer quickened his beat, and to the accompaniment of a long-drawn rattle, the banners leapt up, furled and fluttering, into the air.

To the stranger who has never seen a Palio these little dress rehearsals are richly promising and exciting. Charmed by these present hints, he looks forward eagerly to what the day itself holds in store. Even the Sienese are excited. The pageant, however familiar, does not pall on them. And all the gambler in them, all the local patriot looks forward to the result of the race. Those last days of June before the first Palio, that middle week of August before the second, are days of growing excitement and tension in Siena. One enjoys the Palio the more for having lived through them.

Even the mayor and corporation are infected by the pervading excitement. They are so far carried away that, in the last days of June, they send a small army of men down in the great square before the Palazzo Comunale to eradicate every blade of grass or tuft of moss that can be found growing in the crannies between the flag-stones. It amounts almost to a national characteristic, this hatred of growing things among the works of men. I have often, in old Italian towns, seen workmen laboriously weeding the less frequented streets and squares. The Colosseum, mantled till thirty or forty years ago with a romantic, Piranesian growth of shrubs, grasses and flowers, was officially weeded with such extraordinary energy that its ruinousness was sensibly increased. More stones were brought down in those few months of weeding than had fallen of their own accord in the previous thousand years. But the Italians were pleased ; which is, after all, the chief thing that matters. Their hatred of weeds is fostered by their national pride ; a great country, and one which specially piques itself on being modern, cannot allow weeds to grow even among its ruins. I entirely understand and sympathize with the Italian point of view. If Mr. Ruskin and his disciples had talked about my house and me as they talked about Italy and the Italians, I too should pique myself on being up-to-date ; I should put in bathrooms, central heating and a lift, I should have all the moss scratched off the walls, I should lay cork lino on the marble floors.   Indeed, I think that I should probably, in my irritation, pull down the whole house and build a new one.   Considering the provocation they have received, it seems to me that the Italians have been re-markably moderate in the matter of weeding, destroying and rebuilding.   Their moderation is due in part, no doubt, to their comparative poverty.   Their ancestors built with such pro-digious solidity that it would cost as much to pull down one of their old houses as to build a new one.   Imagine, for example, demolishing the Palazzo Strozzi in Florence.   It would be about as easy to demolish the Matterhorn.   In Rome, which is predominantly a baroque, seventeenth-century city, the houses are made of flimsier stuff.   Consequently, modernization progresses there much more rapidly than in most other Italian towns.   In wealthier England very little an-tiquity has been permitted to stand.   Thus, most of the great country houses of England were rebuilt during the eighteenth century.   If Italy had preserved her independence and her prosperity during the seventeenth, eighteenth and nineteenth centuries, there would probably be very much less mediaeval or renaissance work now surviving than is actually the case.   Money, then, is lacking to modernize completely.   Weeding has the merit of being cheap and, at the same time, richly symbolic.   When you say of a town that the grass grows in its streets, you mean that it is utterly dead.   Conversely, if there is no grass in its streets, it must be alive.   No doubt the mayor and corporation of Siena did not put the argument quite so explicitly.   But that the argument was put, somehow, obscurely and below the surface of the mind, I do not doubt.   The weeding was symbolic of modernity.

With the weeders came other workmen who built up round the curving flanks of the great piazza a series of wooden stands, six tiers high, for the spectators.   The piazza which is shaped, whether by accident or design I do not know, like an ancient theatre, became for the time being indeed a theatre.   Between the seats and the central area of the place, a track was railed off and the slippery flags covered parsimoniously with sand.   Expectation rose higher than ever.

And at last the day came.   The swallows and

swifts wove their arabesques as usual in the bright golden light above the town. But their shrill crying was utterly inaudible, through the deep, continuous, formless murmur of the crowd that thronged the streets and the great piazza. Under its canopy of stone the great bell of the Mangia tower swung incessantly backwards and forwards; it too seemed dumb. The talking, the laughter, the shouting of forty thousand people rose up from the piazza in a column of solid sound, impenetrable to any ordinary noise.

It was after six. We took our places in one of the stands opposite the Palazzo Comunale. Our side of the piazza was already in the shade; but the sun still shone on the palace and its tall slender tower, making their rosy brickwork glow as though by inward fire. An immense concourse of people filled the square and all the tiers of seats round it. There were people in every window, even on the roofs. At the Derby, on boat-race days, at Wembley I have seen larger crowds; but never, I think, so many people confined within so small a space.

The sound of a gunshot broke through the noise of voices; and at the signal a company of mounted carabiniers rode into the piazza, driving the loungers who still thronged the track before them. They were in full dress uniform, black and red, with silver trimmings ; cocked hats on their heads and swords in their hands. On their handsome little horses, they looked like a squadron of smart Napoleonic cavalry. The idlers retreated before them, squeezing their way through every convenient opening in the rails into the central area, which was soon densely packed. The track was cleared at a walk and, cleared, was rounded again at the trot, dashingly, in the best Carle Vernet style. The carabiniers got their applause and retired. The crowd waited expectantly. For a moment there was almost a silence. The bell on the tower ceased to be dumb. Some one in the crowd let loose a couple of balloons. They mounted perpendicularly into the still air, a red sphere and a purple. They passed out of the shadow into the sunlight ; and the red became a ruby, the purple a glowing amethyst. When they had risen above the level of the roofs, a little breeze caught them and carried them away, still mounting all the time, over our heads, out of sight.

There was another gunshot and Vernet was exchanged for Pinturicchio. The noise of the crowd grew louder as they appeared, the bell swung, but gave no sound, and across the square

the trumpets of the procession were all but inaudible. Slowly they marched round, the repre-
sentatives of all the seventeen *contrade* of the city.
Besides its drummer and its two bannermen, each
contrada had a man-at-arms on horseback, three
or four halbardiers and young pages and, if it
happened to be one of the ten competing in the
race, a jockey, all of them wearing the Pinturicchian livery in its own particular colours. Their
progress was slow ; for at every fifty paces they
stopped, to allow the bannermen to give an exhibition of their skill with the flags. They must
have taken the best part of an hour to get round.
But the time seemed only too short. The Palio
is a spectacle of which one does not grow tired.
I have seen it three times now and was as much
delighted on the last occasion as on the first.

English tourists are often sceptical about the
Palio. They remember those terrible ' pageants '
which were all the rage some fifteen years ago in
their own country, and they imagine that the
Palio will turn out to be something of the same
sort. But let me reassure them ; it is not.
There is no poetry by Louis Napoleon Parker at
Siena. There are no choruses of young ladies
voicing high moral sentiments in low voices.
There are no flabby actor-managers imperfectly

disguised as Hengist and Horsa, no crowd of
gesticulating supernumeraries dressed in the worst
of taste and the cheapest of bunting. Nor finally
does one often meet at Siena with that almost
invariable accompaniment of the English pageant
—rain. No, the Palio is just a show ; having
no ' meaning ' in particular, but by the mere fact
of being traditional and still alive, signifying infinitely more than the dead-born English affairs
for all their Parkerian blank verse and their dramatic re-evocations. For these pages and men-at-
arms and bannermen come straight out of the
Pinturicchian past. Their clothes are those designed for their ancestors, copied faithfully, once
in a generation, in the same colours and the same
rich materials. They walk, not in cotton or
flannelette, but in silks and furs and velvets. And
the colours were matched, the clothes originally
cut by men whose taste was the faultless taste
of the early renaissance. To be sure there are
costumiers with as good a taste in these days.
But it was not Paquin, not Lanvin or Poiret who
dressed the actors of the English pageants ; it was
professional wig-makers and lady amateurs. I
have already spoken of the beauty of the flags—
the bold, fantastic, ' modern ' design of them.
Everything else at the Palio is in keeping with

the flags, daring, brilliant and yet always right, always irreproachably refined. The one false note is always the *Palio* itself—the painted banner which is given to the *contrada* whose horse wins the race. This banner is specially painted every year for the occasion. Look at it, where it comes along, proudly exposed on the great mediaeval war chariot which closes the procession—look at it, or preferably don't look at it. It is a typical property from the wardrobe of an English pageant committee. It is a lady amateur's masterpiece. Shuddering, one averts the eyes.

Preceded by a line of *quattrocento* pages carrying festoons of laurel leaves and escorted by a company of mounted knights, the war chariot rolled slowly and ponderously past, bearing aloft the unworthy trophy. And by now the trumpets at the head of the procession sounded, almost inaudibly for us, from the further side of the piazza. And at last the whole procession had made its round and was lined up in close order in front of the Palazzo Comunale. Over the heads of the spectators standing in the central area, we could see all the thirty-four banners waving and waving in a last concerted display and at last, together, all leaping high into the air, hesitating at the top of their leap, falling back, out of sight.

There was a burst of applause. The pageant was over. Another gunshot. And in the midst of more applause, the racehorses were ridden to the starting place.

The course is three times round the piazza, whose shape, as I have said, is something like that of an ancient theatre. Consequently, there are two sharp turns, where the ends of the semicircle meet the straight diameter. One of these, owing to the irregularity of the plan, is sharper than the other. The outside wall of the track is padded with mattresses at this point, to prevent impetuous jockeys who take the corner too fast from dashing themselves to pieces. The jockeys ride bareback ; the horses run on a thin layer of sand spread over the flagstones of the piazza. The Palio is probably the most dangerous flat-race in the world. And it is made the more dangerous by the excessive patriotism of the rival *contrade*. For the winner of the race as he reins in his horse after passing the post, is set upon by the supporters of the other *contrade* (who all think that *their* horse should have won), with so real and earnest a fury that the carabiniers must always intervene to protect man and beast from lynching. Our places were at a point some two or three hundred yards beyond the post, so that we had an excellent view of the battle waged round the winning horse, as he slackened speed. Scarcely was the post passed when the crowd broke its ranks and rushed out into the course. Still cantering, the horse came up the track. A gang of young men ran in pursuit, waving sticks and shouting. And with them, their Napoleonic coat tails streaming in the wind of their own speed, their cocked hats bobbing, and brandishing swords in their white-gloved hands, ran the rescuing carabiniers. There was a brief struggle round the now stationary horse, the young men were repulsed, and surrounded by cocked hats, followed by a crowd of supporters from its native *contrada*, the beast was led off in triumph. We climbed down from our places. The piazza was now entirely shaded It was only on the upper part of the tower and the battlements of the great Palazzo that the sun still shone. Rosily against the pale blue sky, they glowed. The swifts still turned and turned overhead in the light. It is said that at evening and at dawn these light-loving birds mount on their strong wings into the sky to bid a last farewell or earliest good-morrow to the sinking or the rising sun. While we lie sleeping or have resigned ourselves to darkness the swifts are looking down from their watch-tower in the height of heaven over the edge of the turning planet towards the light. Was it a fable, I wondered, looking up at the wheeling birds? Or was it true? Meanwhile, some one was swearing at me for not looking where I was going. I postponed the speculation.

I HAVE always been rather partial to plane geometry ; probably because it was the only branch of mathematics that was ever taught me in such a way that I could understand it. For though I have no belief in the power of education to turn public school boys into Newtons (it being quite obvious that, whatever opportunity may be offered, it is only those rare beings desirous of learning and possessing a certain amount of native ability who ever do learn anything), yet I must insist, in my own defence, that the system of mathematical instruction of which, at Eton, I was the unfortunate victim, was calculated not merely to turn my desire to learn into stubborn passive resistance, but also to stifle whatever rudimentary aptitude in this direction I might have possessed. But let that pass. Suffice to say that, in spite of my education and my congenital ineptitude, plane geometry has always charmed me by its simplicity and elegance, its elimination of detail and the individual case, its insistence on generalities.

My love for plane geometry prepared me to feel a special affection for Holland. For the Dutch landscape has all the qualities that make

geometry so delightful   A tour in Holland is a
tour through the first books of Euclid.   Over a
country that is the ideal plane surface of the
geometry books, the roads and the canals trace
out the shortest distances between point and point.
In the interminable polders, the road-topped
dykes and gleaming ditches intersect one another
at right angles, a criss-cross of perfect parallels.
Each rectangle of juicy meadowland contained
between the intersecting dykes has identically the
same area.   Five kilometres long, three deep—
the figures record themselves on the clock face of
the cyclometer.   Five by three by—how many ?
The demon of calculation possesses the mind.
Rolling along those smooth brick roads between
the canals, one strains one's eyes to count the
dykes at right angles and parallel to one's own.
One calculates the area of the polders they enclose.   So many square kilometres.   But the
square kilometres have to be turned into acres.
It is a fearful sum to do in one's head ; the more
so as one has forgotten how many square yards
there are in an acre.

And all the time, as one advances the huge
geometrical landscape spreads out on either side
of the car like an opening fan.   Along the level
sky-line a score of windmills wave their arms like

dancers in a geometrical ballet. Ineluctably, the laws of perspective lead away the long roads and shining waters to a misty vanishing point. Here and there—mere real irrelevancies in the midst of this ideal plain—a few black and white cows out of a picture by Cuyp browse indefatigably in the lush green grass or, remembering Paul Potter, mirror themselves like so many ruminating Narcissi, in the waters of a canal. Sometimes one passes a few human beings, deplorably out of place, but doing their best, generally, to make up for their ungeometrical appearance by mounting bicycles. The circular wheels suggest a variety of new theorems and a new task for the demon of calculation. Suppose the radius of the wheels to be fifteen inches ; then fifteen times fifteen times *pi* will be the area. The only trouble is that one has forgotten the value of *pi*.

Hastily I exorcise the demon of calculation that I may be free to admire the farm-house on the opposite bank of the canal on our right. How perfectly it fits into the geometrical scheme ! On a cube, cut down to about a third of its height, is placed a tall pyramid. That is the house. A plantation of trees, set in quincunx formation, surrounds it ; the limits of its rectangular garden are drawn in water on the green plain, and beyond these neat ditches extend the interminable flat fields. There are no outhouses, no barns, no farm-yard with untidy stacks. The hay is stored under the huge pyramidal roof, and in the truncated cube below live, on one side the farmer and his family, on the other side (during winter only ; for during the rest of the year they sleep in the fields) his black and white Cuyp cows. Every farm-house in North Holland conforms to this type, which is traditional, and so perfectly fitted to the landscape that it would have been impossible to devise anything more suitable. An English farm with its ranges of straggling buildings, its untidy yard, full of animals, its haystacks and pigeon-cotes would be horribly out of place here. In the English landscape, which is all accidents, variety, detail and particular cases, it is perfect. But here, in this generalized and Euclidean North Holland, it would be a blot and a discord. Geometry calls for geometry ; with a sense of the aesthetic proprieties which one cannot too highly admire, the Dutch have responded to the appeal of the landscape and have dotted the plane surface of their country with cubes and pyramids.

Delightful landscape ! I know of no country that it is more mentally exhilarating to travel in.

No wonder Descartes preferred the Dutch to any other scene. It is the rationalist's paradise. One feels as one flies along in the teeth of one's own forty-mile-an-hour wind like a Cartesian Encyclopaedist—flushed with mental intoxication, convinced that Euclid is absolute reality, that God is a mathematician, that the universe is a simple affair that can be explained in terms of physics and mechanics, that all men are equally endowed with reason and that it is only a question of putting the right arguments before them to make them see the error of their ways and to inaugurate the reign of justice and common sense. Those were noble and touching dreams, commendable inebriations ! We are soberer now. We have learnt that nothing is simple and rational except what we ourselves have invented ; that God thinks neither in terms of Euclid nor of Riemann ; that science has ' explained ' nothing ; that the more we know the more fantastic the world becomes and the profounder the surrounding darkness ; that reason is unequally distributed ; that instinct is the sole source of action ; that prejudice is incomparably stronger than argument and that even in the twentieth century men behave as they did in the caves of Altamira and in the lake dwellings of Glastonbury. And symbolically one makes the same discoveries in Holland. For the polders are not unending, nor all the canals straight, nor every house a wedded cube and pyramid, nor even the fundamental plane surface invariably plane. That delightful ' Last Ride Together ' feeling that fills one, as one rolls along the brick-topped dykes between the canals is deceptive. The present is not eternal ; the ' Last Ride ' through plane geometry comes to a sudden end—in a town, in forests, in the sea coast, in a winding river or great estuary. It matters little which ; all are fundamentally ungeometrical ; each has power to dissipate in an instant all those ' paralogisms of rationalism ' (as Professor Rougier calls them) which we have so fondly cherished among the polders. The towns have crooked streets thronged with people ; the houses are of all shapes and sizes. The coast-line is not straight nor regularly curved and its dunes or its dykes (for it must be defended against the besieging waves by art if not by nature) rear themselves inexcusably out of the plane surface. The woods are unscientific in their shady mysteriousness and one cannot see them for all their individual trees. The rivers are tortuous and alive with boats and barges. The inlets of the sea are entirely shapeless. It is the real world again after the ideal—hopelessly diversified, complex and obscure ; but, when the first regrets are over, equally charming with the geometrical landscape we have left behind. We shall find it more charming, indeed, if our minds are practical and extroverted. Personally, I balance my affections. For I love the inner world as much as the outer. When the outer vexes me, I retire to the rational simplicities of the inner—to the polders of the spirit. And when, in their turn, the polders seem unduly flat, the roads too straight and the laws of perspective too tyrannous, I emerge again into the pleasing confusion of untempered reality.

And how beautiful, how curious in Holland that confusion is ! I think of Rotterdam with its enormous river and its great bridges, so crowded with the traffic of a metropolis that one has to wait in files, half a mile long, for one's turn to cross. I think of The Hague and how it tries to be elegant and only succeeds in being respectable and upper middle class ; of Delft, the commercial city of three hundred years ago ; of Haarlem where, in autumn, you see them carting bulbs as in other countries they cart potatoes ; of Hoorn on the Zuyder Zee, with its little harbour and seaward-looking castle, its absurd museum filled with rich mixed rubbish, its huge storehouse of cheeses, like an old-fashioned arsenal, where the workmen are busy all day long polishing the yellow cannon balls on a kind of lathe and painting them bright pink with an aniline stain. I think of Volendam—one line of wooden houses perched on the sea wall, and another line crouching in the low green fields behind the dyke. The people at Volendam are dressed as for a musical comedy—*Miss Hook of Holland*—the men in baggy trousers and short jackets, the women in winged white caps, tight bodices, and fifteen superimposed petticoats. Five thousand tourists come daily to look at them ; but they still, by some miracle, retain their independence and self-respect. I think of Amsterdam ; the old town, like a livelier Bruges, mirrors its high brick houses in the canals. In one quarter an enormous courtesan sits smiling at every window, the meatiest specimens of humanity I ever saw At nine in the morning, at lunch-time, at six in the afternoon, the streets are suddenly filled with three hundred thousand bicycles ; every one, in Amsterdam, goes to and from his business on a pair of wheels. For the pedestrian as well as for the motorist it is a nightmare. And they are all trick cyclists. Children of four carry children of three on their

III

SALEM COLLEGE LIBRARY
Winston-Salem North Carolina

handle-bars. Mothers pedal gaily along with month-old infants sleeping in cradles fastened to the back carrier. Messenger boys think nothing of taking two cubic metres of parcels. Dairymen do their rounds on bicycles specially constructed to accommodate two hundred quart bottles of milk in a tray between the two wheels. I have seen nursery gardeners carrying four palms and a dozen of potted chrysanthemums on their handle-bars. I have seen five people riding through the traffic on one machine. The most daring feats of the circus and the music hall are part of the quotidian routine in Amsterdam.

I think of the dunes near Schoorl. Seen from a little distance across the plain they look like a range of enormous mountains against the sky. Following with the eye that jagged silhouette one can feel all the emotions aroused, shall we say, by the spectacle of the Alps seen from Turin. The dunes are grand ; one could write a canto from *Childe Harold* about them. And then, unfortunately, one realizes what for a moment one had forgotten, that this line of formidable peaks is not looking down at one from fifty miles away, over the curving flank of the planet ; it is just a furlong distant, and the chimneys of the houses at its base reach nearly two-thirds of the way to the top. But what does that matter ? With a little good will, I insist, one can feel in Holland all the emotions appropriate to Switzerland.

Yes, they are grand, the dunes of Schoorl and Groet But I think the grandest sight I saw in non-geometrical Holland was Zaandam—Zaandam from a distance, across the plain.

We had been driving through the polders and the open country of North Holland. Zaandam was the first piece of ungeometrical reality since Alkmaer. Technically, Zaandam is not picturesque ; the guide-book has little to say about it. It is a port and manufacturing town on the Zaan, a few miles north of Amsterdam ; that is all. They make cocoa there and soap. The air at Zaandam is charged in alternative strata with delicious vapours of molten chocolate and the stench of boiling fat. In wharves by the shores of the river they store American grain and timber from the Baltic. It was the granaries that first announced, from a distance, the presence of Zaandam. Like the cathedrals of a new religion, yet unpreached, they towered up into the hazy autumn air—huge oblongs of concrete set on end, almost windowless, smooth and blankly grey. It was as though their whole force were directed vertically upwards ; to look from windows horizontally across the world would have been a distraction ; eyes were sacrificed to this upward purpose. And the direction of that purpose was emphasized by the lines of the alternately raised and lowered panels into which the wall spaces of the great buildings were divided—long fine lines of shadow running up unbrokenly through a hundred feet from base to summit. The builders of the papal palace at Avignon used a very similar device to give their castle its appearance of enormous height and formidable impendence. The raised panel and the shallow blind arches, impossibly long in the leg, with which they variegated the surface of the wall, impart to the whole building an impetuous upward tendency. It is the same with the grain elevators at Zaandam. In the haze of autumnal Holland I remembered Provence. And I remembered, as I watched those towering shapes growing larger and larger as we approached, Chartres and Bourges and Reims : gigantic silhouettes seen at the end of a day's driving, towards evening, against a pale sky, with the little lights of a city about their base.

But if at a distance, Zaandam, by its commercial monuments, reminds one of Provençal castles and the Gothic cathedrals of France, a nearer view proclaims it to be unequivocally Dutch. At the

foot of the elevators and the only less enormous
factories, in the atmosphere of chocolate and soap,
lies the straggling town   The suburbs are long,
but narrow ; for they cling precariously to a
knife-edge of land between two waters   The
houses are small, made of wood and gaudily
painted ; with gardens as large as table-cloths,
beautifully kept and filled—at any rate at the
season when I saw them—with plushy begonias.
In one, as large, in this case, as two table-cloths,
were no less than fourteen large groups of statu-
ary.   In the streets are men in wooden shoes,
smoking.   Dogs drawing carts with brass pots in
them.   Innumerable bicycles.   It is the real and
not the ideal geometrical Holland, crowded, con-
fusing, various, odd, charming. . . . But I sighed as
we entered the town.   The 'Last Ride Together'
was over ; the dear paralogisms of rationalism
were left behind.   It was now necessary to face
the actual world of men—and to face it, in my
case, with precisely five words of Dutch (and
patois at that) learned years before for the benefit
of a Flemish servant : ' Have you fed the cat ? '
No wonder I regretted the polders.

'THEY call it the Palazzo del Te,' said the
maid at the little inn in the back street where we
had lunch, ' because the Gonzaga used to go and
take tea there.' And that was all that she, and
probably most of the other inhabitants of Mantua,
knew about the Gonzaga or their palaces. It
was surprising, perhaps, that she should have
known so much. Gonzaga—the name, at least,
still faintly reverberated. After two hundred
years, how many names are still remembered ?
Few indeed. The Gonzaga, it seemed to me,
enjoy a degree of immortality that might be
envied them. They have vanished, they are as
wholly extinct as the dinosaur ; but in the cities
they once ruled their name still vaguely echoes,
and for those who care to listen they have left
behind some of the most eloquent sermons on the
vanity of human wishes and the mutability of
fortune that stones have ever mutely preached.

I have seen many ruins and of every period.
Stonehenge and Ansedonia, Ostia and mediaeval
Ninfa (which the duke of Sermoneta is busily
turning into the likeness of a neat suburban park),
Bolsover and the gruesome modern ruins in
Northern France. I have seen great cities dead

or in decay : Pisa, Bruges and the newly murdered Vienna. But over none, it seemed to me,
did there brood so profound a melancholy as over
Mantua ; none seemed so dead or so utterly
bereft of glory ; nowhere was desolation more
pregnant with the memory of splendour, the
silence nowhere so richly musical with echoes.
There are a thousand rooms in the labyrinthine
Reggia at Mantua—Gothic rooms, rooms of
the renaissance, baroque rooms, rooms rich with
the absurd pretentious decorations of the first
empire, huge presence chambers and closets and
the horribly exquisite apartments of the dwarfs—
a thousand rooms, and their walls enclose an
emptiness that is the mournful ghost of departed
plenitude. It is through Mallarmé's *creux néant
musicien* that one walks in Mantua.

And not in Mantua alone. For wherever the
Gonzaga lived, they left behind them the same
pathetic emptiness, the same pregnant desolation,
the same echoes, the same ghosts of splendour.

The Palazzo del Te is made sad and beautiful
with the same melancholy as broods in the Reggia.
True, the stupid vulgarity of Giulio Romano was
permitted to sprawl over its wall in a series of
deplorable frescoes (it is curious, by the way, that
Giulio Romano should have been the only Italian

117

artist of whom Shakespeare had ever heard, or at least the only one he ever mentioned) ; but the absurdities and grossnesses seem actually to make the place more touching. The departed tenants of the palace become in a manner more real to one, when one discovers that their taste ran to *trompe l'œil* pictures of fighting giants and mildly pornographic scenes out of pagan mythology. And seeming more human, they seem also more dead ; and the void left by their disappearance is more than ever musical with sadness.

Even the cadets of the Gonzaga house enjoyed a power of leaving behind them a more than Pompeian desolation. Twenty miles from Mantua, on the way to Cremona, is a village called Sabbioneta. It lies near the Po, though not on its banks ; possesses, for a village, a tolerably large population, mostly engaged in husbandry ; is rather dirty and has an appearance—probably quite deceptive—of poverty. In fact it is just like all other villages of the Lombard plain, but with this difference : a Gonzaga once lived here. The squalor of Sabbioneta is no common squalor ; it is a squalor that was once magnificence. Its farmers and horse-copers live, dirtily and destructively, in treasures of late renaissance architecture. The town hall is a ducal palace ; in the municipal school, children are taught under carved and painted ceilings, and when the master is out of the room they write their names on the marble bellies of the patient, battered caryatids who uphold the scutcheoned mantel. The weekly cinema show is given in an Olympic theatre, built a few years after the famous theatre at Vicenza, by Palladio's pupil, Scamozzi. The people worship in sumptuous churches, and if ever soldiers happen to pass through the town, they are billeted in the deserted summer palace.

The creator of all these splendours was Vespasiano, son of that Luigi Gonzaga, the boon companion of kings, whom, for his valour and his fabulous strength, his contemporaries nicknamed Rodomonte. Luigi died young, killed in battle; and his son Vespasiano was brought up by his aunt, Giulia Gonzaga, one of the most perfectly courtly ladies of her age. She had him taught Latin, Greek, the mathematics, good manners and the art of war. This last he practised with distinction, serving at one time or another under many princes, but chiefly under Philip II. of Spain, who honoured him with singular favours. Vespasiano seems to have been the typical Italian tyrant of his period—cultured, intelligent and only just so much of an ungovernably ferocious ruffian as one would expect a man to be who has been brought up in the possession of absolute power. It was in the intimacy of private life that he displayed his least amiable characteristics. He poisoned his first wife on a suspicion, probably unfounded, of her infidelity, murdered her supposed lover and exiled his relations. His second wife left him mysteriously after three years of married life and died of pure misery in a convent, carrying with her into the grave nobody knew what frightful secret. His third wife, it is true, lived to a ripe old age; but then Vespasiano himself died after only a few years of marriage. His only son, whom he loved with the anxious passion of the ambitious parvenu who desires to found a dynasty, one day annoyed him by not taking off his cap when he met him in the street. Vespasiano rebuked him for this lack of respect. The boy answered back impertinently. Whereupon Vespasiano gave him such a frightful kick in the groin that the boy died. Which shows that, even when chastising one's own children, it is advisable to observe the Queensberry rules.

It was in 1560 that Vespasiano decided to convert the miserable village from which he took his title into a capital worthy of its ruler. He set to work with energy. In a few years the village of

squalid cottages clustering round a feudal castle
had given place to a walled town, with broad
streets, two fine squares, a couple of palaces and
a noble Gallery of Antiques. These last Vespasiano had inherited from his father, Rodomonte,
who had been at the sack of Rome in 1527 and
had shown himself an industrious and discriminating looter. Sabbioneta was in its turn looted by
the Austrians, who carried off Rodomonte's spoils
to Mantua. The museum remains ; but there
is nothing in it but the *creux néant musicien* which
the Gonzaga alone, of all the princes in Italy, had
the special art of creating by their departure.

We had come to Sabbioneta from Parma. In
the vast Farnese palace there is no musically
echoing void—merely an ordinary, undisturbing
emptiness. Only in the colossal Estensian theatre
does one recapture anything like the Mantuan
melancholy. We drove through Colorno, where
the last of the Este built a summer palace about as
large as Hampton Court. Over the Po, by a
bridge of boats, through Casalmaggiore and on,
tortuously, by little by-roads across the plain. A
line of walls presented themselves, a handsome
gate. We drove in, and immediately faint
ghostly oboes began to play around us ; we were
in Sabbioneta among the Gonzaga ghosts.

The central piazza of the town is oblong; Vespasiano's palace stands at one of the shorter ends, presenting to the world a modest façade, five windows wide, once rich with decorations, but now bare. It serves at present as town hall. In the waiting-room on the first floor, stand four life-sized equestrian figures, carved in wood and painted, representing four of Vespasiano's ancestors. Once there was a squadron of twelve; but the rest have been broken up and burned. This crime, together with all the other ravages committed by time or vandals in the course of three centuries, was attributed by the mayor, who personally did us the honours of his municipality, to the socialists who had preceded him in office. It is unnecessary to add that he himself was a fascista.

We walked round in the emptiness under the superbly carved and gilded ceilings. The porter sat among decayed frescoes in the Cabinet of Diana. The town council held its meetings in the Ducal Saloon. The Gallery of the Ancestors housed a clerk and the municipal archives. The deputy mayor had his office in the Hall of the Elephants. The Sala d'Oro had been turned into an infants' class-room. We walked out again into the sunlight fairly heart-broken.

The Olympic Theatre is a few yards down the street. Accompanied by the obliging young porter from the Cabinet of Diana, we entered. It is a tiny theatre, but complete and marvellously elegant. From the pit, five semicircular steps rise to a pillared loggia, behind which—having the width of the whole auditorium—is the ducal box. The loggia consists of twelve Corinthian pillars, topped by a cornice. On the cornice, above each pillar, stand a dozen stucco gods and goddesses. Noses and fingers, paps and ears have gone the way of all art ; but the general form of them survives. Their white silhouettes gesticulate elegantly against the twilight of the hall.

The stage was once adorned with a fixed scene in perspective, like that which Palladio built at Vicenza. The mayor wanted us to believe that it was his Bolshevik predecessors who had destroyed it ; but as a matter of fact it was taken down about a century ago. Gone, too, are the frescoes with which the walls were once covered. One year of epidemic the theatre was used as a fever hospital. When the plague had passed, it was thought that the frescoes needed disinfecting ; they were thickly white-washed. There is no money to scrape the white-wash off again.

We followed the young porter out of the theatre. Another two or three hundred yards and we were in the Piazza d'Armi. It is an oblong, grassy space. On the long axis of the rectangle, near one end there stands, handsomely pedestalled, a fluted marble column, topped by a statue of Athena, the tutelary goddess of Vespasiano's metropolis. The pedestal, the capital and the statue are of the late renaissance. But the column is antique, and formed a part of Rodomonte's Roman booty. Rodomonte was evidently no petty thief. If a thing is worth doing it is worth doing thoroughly ; that, evidently, was his motto.

One of the long sides of the rectangle is occupied by the Gallery of Antiques. It is a superb building, architecturally by far the finest thing in the town. The lower storey consists of an open arcade and the walls of the gallery above are ornamented with blind arches, having well-proportioned windows at the centre of each and separated from one another by Tuscan pilasters. A very bold projecting cornice, topped by a low roof, finishes the design, which for sober and massive elegance is one of the most remarkable of its kind with which I am acquainted.

The opposite side of the piazza is open, a hedge

separating it from the back gardens of the neighbouring houses. It was here, I fancy, that the
feudal castle originally stood. It was pulled
down, however, during the eighteenth century
(busy Bolsheviks !) and its bricks employed, more
usefully but less aesthetically, to strengthen
the dykes which defend the surrounding plain,
none too impregnably, from the waters of
the Po.

Its destruction has left Vespasiano's summer
palace, or Palace of the Garden, isolated (save
where it joins the Gallery of the Antiques), and
rather forlorn at the end of the long piazza. It
is a long, low building of only two storeys, rather
insignificant from outside. It is evident that
Vespasiano built it as economically as he could.
For him the place was only a week-end cottage,
a holiday resort, whither he could escape from the
metropolitan splendour and bustle of the palace in
the market-place, a quarter of a mile away. Like
all other rulers of small states, Vespasiano must
have found it extremely difficult to take an effective holiday. He could not go ten miles in any
direction without coming to a frontier. Within
his dominions it was impossible to have a change
of air. Wisely, therefore, he decided to concentrate his magnificences. He built his Balmoral

within five minutes' walk of his Buckingham Palace.

We knocked at the door. The caretaker who opened to us was an old woman who might have gone on to any stage and acted Juliet's Nurse without a moment's rehearsal. Within the first two minutes of our acquaintance with her she confided to us that she had just got married—for the third time, at the age of seventy. Her comments on the connubial state were so very Juliet's Nurse, so positively Wife-of-Bath, that we were made to feel quite early-Victorian in comparison with this robustious old gammer from the *quattrocento*. After having told us all that can be told (and much that cannot be told, at any rate in polite society) about the married state, she proceeded to do us the honours of the house. She led the way, opening the shutters of each room in the long suite, as we entered it. And as the light came in through the unglazed windows, what Gonzagesque ravishments were revealed to us. There was a Cabinet of Venus, with the remains of voluptuous nudes, a Hall of the Winds with puffing cherubs and a mantel in red marble ; a Cabinet of the Caesars, floored with marble and adorned with medallions of all the ruffians of antiquity ; a Hall of the Myths on whose ceiling, vaulted into the likeness of a truncated pyramid seen from within, were five delightful scenes from Lemprière—an Icarus, an Apollo and Marsyas, a Phaeton, an Arachne and, in the midst, a to me somewhat mysterious scene : a naked beauty sitting on the back, not of a bull (that would have been simple enough), but of a reclining horse, which turns its head amorously towards her, while she caresses its neck.   Who was the lady and who the travestied god I do not rightly know.   Vague memories of an escapade of Saturn's float through my mind.   But perhaps I am slandering a respectable deity.

But in any case, whatever its subject, the picture is charming.   Vespasiano's principal artist was Bernardino Campi of Cremona.   He was not a good painter, of course ; but at least he was gracefully and charmingly, instead of vulgarly mediocre, like Giulio Romano. About the Palazzo del Te there hangs a certain faded frightfulness ; but the Giardino is all sweetness—mannered, no doubt, and rather feeble—but none the less authentic in its ruinous decay.

The old caretaker expounded the pictures to us as we went round—not out of any knowledge of what they represented, but purely out of her

imagination, which was a good deal more interesting. In the Hall of the Graces, where the
walls are adorned with what remains of a series
of very pretty little *grotteschi* in the Pompeian
manner, her fancy surpassed itself. These, she
said, were the records of the Duke's dreams.
Each time he dreamed a dream he sent for his
painter and had it drawn on the walls of this room.
These—she pointed to a pair of Chimaeras—he
saw in a nightmare ; these dancing satyrs visited
his sleep after a merry evening ; these four urns
were dreamt of after too much wine. As for
the three naked Graces, from whom the room
takes its name, as for those—over the Graces
she once more became too Wife-of-Bath to be
recorded.

Her old cracked laughter went echoing down
the empty rooms ; and it seemed to precipitate
and crystallize all the melancholy suspended, as it
were, in solution within those bleared and peeling
walls. The sense of desolation, vaguely felt
before, became poignant. And when the old
woman ushered us into another room, dark and
smelling of mould like the rest, and threw open
the shutters and called what the light revealed the
' Hall of the Mirrors,' I could almost have wept.
For in the Hall of the Mirrors there are no more

mirrors, only the elaborate framing of them on walls and ceiling. Where the glasses of Murano once shone are spaces of bare plaster that stare out like blind eyes, blankly and, it seems after a little, reproachfully. 'They used to dance in this room,' said the old woman.

Part III
WORKS OF ART

BREUGHEL

Most of our mistakes are fundamentally grammatical. We create our own difficulties by employing an inadequate language to describe facts. Thus, to take one example, we are constantly giving the same name to more than one thing, and more than one name to the same thing. The results, when we come to argue, are deplorable. For we are using a language which does not adequately describe the things about which we are arguing.

The word 'painter' is one of those names whose indiscriminate application has led to the worst results. All those who, for whatever reason and with whatever intentions, put brushes to canvas and make pictures, are called without distinction, painters. Deceived by the uniqueness of the name, aestheticians have tried to make us believe that there is a single painter-psychology, a single function of painting, a single standard of criticism. Fashion changes and the views of art critics with it. At the present time it is fashionable to believe in form to the exclusion of subject. Young people almost swoon away with excess of aesthetic emotion before a Matisse. Two generations ago they would have been wiping their eyes before the latest Landseer. (Ah, those more than human, those positively Christ-like dogs— how they moved, what lessons they taught! There had been no religious painting like Land- seer's since Carlo Dolci died.)

These historical considerations should make us chary of believing too exclusively in any single theory of art. One kind of painting, one set of ideas are fashionable at any given moment. They are made the basis of a theory which condemns all other kinds of painting and all preceding critical theories. The process con- stantly repeats itself.

At the present moment, it is true, we have achieved an unprecedently tolerant eclecticism. We are able, if we are up-to-date, to enjoy every- thing, from negro sculpture to Lucca della Robbia and from Magnasco to Byzantine mosaics. But it is an eclecticism achieved at the expense of almost the whole content of the various works of art considered. What we have learned to see in all these works is their formal qualities, which we abstract and arbitrarily call essential. The sub- ject of the work, with all that the painter desired to express in it beyond his feelings about formal relations, contemporary criticism rejects as unim- portant. The young painter scrupulously avoids

Introducing into his pictures anything that might be mistaken for a story, or the expression of a view of life, while the young *Kunstforscher* turns, as though at an act of exhibitionism, from any manifestation by a contemporary of any such forbidden interest in drama or philosophy. True, the old masters are indulgently permitted to illustrate stories and express their thoughts about the world. Poor devils, they knew no better! Your modern observer makes allowance for their ignorance and passes over in silence all that is not a matter of formal relations. The admirers of Giotto (as numerous to-day as were the admirers of Guido Reni a hundred years ago) contrive to look at the master's frescoes without considering what they represent, or what the painter desired to express. Every germ of drama or meaning is disinfected out of them ; only the composition is admired. The process is analogous to reading Latin verses without understanding them— simply for the sake of the rhythmical rumbling of the hexameters.

It would be absurd, of course, to deny the importance of formal relations. No picture can hold together without composition and no good painter is without some specific passion for form as such—just as no good writer is without a passion for words and the arrangement of words. It is obvious that no man can adequately express himself, unless he takes an interest in the terms which he proposes to use as his medium of expression. Not all painters are interested in the same sort of forms. Some, for example, have a passion for masses and the surfaces of solids. Others delight in lines. Some compose in three dimensions. Others like to make silhouettes on the flat. Some like to make the surface of the paint smooth and, as it were, translucent, so that the objects represented in the picture can be seen distinct and separate, as through a sheet of glass. Others (as for example Rembrandt) love to make a rich thick surface which shall absorb and draw together into one whole all the objects represented, and that in spite of the depth of the composition and the distance of the objects from the plane of the picture. All these purely aesthetic considerations are, as I have said, important. All artists are interested in them ; but almost none are interested in them to the exclusion of everything else. It is very seldom indeed that we find a painter who can be inspired merely by his interest in form and texture to paint a picture. Good painters of ' abstract ' subjects or even of still lives are rare. Apples and solid geometry do not stimulate a man to express his feelings about form and make a composition. All thoughts and emotions are inter-dependent. In the words of the dear old song,

> The roses round the door
> Make me love mother more.

One feeling is excited by another. Our faculties work best in a congenial emotional atmosphere. For example, Mantegna's faculty for making noble arrangements of forms was stimulated by his feelings about heroic and god-like humanity. Expressing those feelings, which he found exciting, he also expressed—and in the most perfect manner of which he was capable—his feelings about masses, surfaces, solids, and voids. 'The roses round the door '—his hero worship—' made him love mother more '—made him, by stimulating his faculty for composition, paint better. If Isabella d'Este had made him paint apples, table napkins and bottles, he would have produced, being uninterested in these objects, a poor composition. And yet, from a purely formal point of view, apples, bottles and napkins are quite as interesting as human bodies and faces. But Mantegna—and with him the majority of painters—did not happen to be very passionately interested in these inanimate objects. When one is bored one becomes boring.

> The apples round the door
> Make me a frightful bore.

Inevitably ; unless I happen to be so exclusively interested in form that I can paint anything that has a shape ; or unless I happen to possess some measure of that queer pantheism, that animistic superstition which made Van Gogh regard the humblest of common objects as being divinely or devilishly alive. ' *Crains dans le mur aveugle un regard qui t'épie.*' If a painter can do that, he will be able, like Van Gogh, to make pictures of cabbage fields and the bedrooms of cheap hotels that shall be as wildly dramatic as a Rape of the Sabines.

The contemporary fashion is to admire beyond all others the painter who can concentrate on the formal side of his art and produce pictures which are entirely devoid of literature. Old Renoir's apophthegm, ' *Un peintre, voyez-vous, qui a le sentiment du téton et des fesses, est un homme sauvé,*' is considered by the purists suspiciously latitudinarian. A painter who has the sentiment of the pap and the buttocks is a painter who portrays real models with gusto. Your pure aesthete should

only have a feeling for hemispheres, curved lines
and surfaces. But this 'sentiment of the buttocks' is common to all good painters. It is the
lowest common measure of the whole profession.
It is possible, like Mantegna, to have a passionate feeling for all that is solid, and at the same
time to be a stoic philosopher and a hero-wor-
shipper; possible, with Michelangelo, to have
a complete realization of breasts and also an
interest in the soul or, like Rubens, to have a
sentiment for human greatness as well as for
human rumps. The greater includes the less;
great dramatic or reflective painters know everything that the aestheticians who paint geometrical
pictures, apples or buttocks know, and a great deal
more besides. What they have to say about
formal relations, though important, is only a part
of what they have to express. The contemporary insistence on form to the exclusion of
everything else is an absurdity. So was the older
insistence on exact imitation and sentiment to the
exclusion of form. There need be no exclusions.
In spite of the single name, there are many
different kinds of painters and all of them, with
the exception of those who cannot paint, and those
whose minds are trivial, vulgar and tedious, have
a right to exist.

139

All classifications and theories are made after the event ; the facts must first occur before they can be tabulated and methodized. Reversing the historical process, we attack the facts forearmed with theoretical prejudice. Instead of considering each fact on its own merits, we ask how it fits into the theoretical scheme. At any given moment a number of meritorious facts fail to fit into the fashionable theory and have to be ignored. Thus El Greco's art failed to conform with the ideal of good painting held by Philip the Second and his contemporaries. The Sienese primitives seemed to the seventeenth and eighteenth centuries incompetent barbarians. Under the influence of Ruskin, the later nineteenth century contrived to dislike almost all architecture that was not Gothic. And the early twentieth century, under the influence of the French, deplores and ignores, in painting, all that is literary, reflective or dramatic.

In every age theory has caused men to like much that was bad and reject much that was good. The only prejudice that the ideal art critic should have is against the incompetent, the mentally dishonest and the futile. The number of ways in which good pictures can be painted is quite incalculable, depending only on the variability of

the human mind.   Every good painter invents a
new way of painting.   Is this man a competent
painter ? Has he something to say, is he genuine ?
These are the questions a critic must ask himself.
Not, Does he conform with my theory of imitation, or distortion, or moral purity, or significant
form ?

There is one painter against whom, it seems to
me, theoretical prejudice has always most un-
fairly told.   I mean the elder Breughel.   Looking at his best paintings I find that I can honestly
answer in the affirmative all the questions which
a critic may legitimately put himself.   He is
highly competent aesthetically ; he has plenty to
say ; his mind is curious, interesting and powerful ; and he has no false pretensions, is entirely
honest.   And yet he has never enjoyed the high
reputation to which his merits entitle him.   This
is due, I think, to the fact that his work has never
quite squared with any of the various critical
theories which since his days have had a vogue
in the aesthetic world.

A subtle colourist, a sure and powerful
draughtsman, and possessing powers of composition that enable him to marshal the innumerable
figures with which his pictures are filled into pleas-
ingly decorative groups (built up, as we see, when

we try to analyse his methods of formal arrangement, out of individually flat, silhouette-like shapes standing in a succession of receding planes), Breughel can boast of purely aesthetic merits that ought to endear him even to the strictest sect of the Pharisees. Coated with this pure aesthetic jam, the bitter pill of his literature might easily, one would suppose, be swallowed. If Giotto's dalliance with sacred history be forgiven him, why may not Breughel be excused for being an anthropologist and a social philosopher? To which I tentatively answer: Giotto is forgiven, because we have so utterly ceased to believe in Catholic Christianity that we can easily ignore the subject matter of his pictures and concentrate only on their formal qualities; Breughel, on the other hand, is unforgivable because he made comments on humanity that are still interesting to us. From his subject matter we cannot escape; it touches us too closely to be ignored. That is why Breughel is despised by all up-to-date *Kunstforschers*.

And even in the past, when there was no theoretical objection to the mingling of literature and painting, Breughel failed, for another reason, to get his due. He was considered low, gross, a mere comedian, and as such unworthy of serious consideration. Thus, the *Encyclopaedia Brit-annica*, which in these matters may be safely relied on to give the current opinion of a couple of generations ago, informs us, in the eleven lines which it parsimoniously devotes to Peter Breughel that ' the subjects of his pictures are chiefly humorous figures, like those of D. Teniers ; and if he wants the delicate touch and silvery clearness of that master, he has abundant spirit and comic power.'

Whoever wrote these words—and they might have been written by any one desirous, fifty years ago, of playing for safety and saying the right thing—can never have taken the trouble to look at any of the pictures painted by Breughel when he was a grown and accomplished artist.

In his youth, it is true, he did a great deal of hack work for a dealer who specialized in caricatures and devils in the manner of Hieronymus Bosch. But his later pictures, painted when he had really mastered the secrets of his art, are not comic at all. They are studies of peasant life, they are allegories, they are religious pictures of the most strangely reflective cast, they are exquisitely poetical landscapes. Breughel died at the height of his powers. But there is enough of his mature work in existence—at Antwerp, at

Brussels, at Naples and above all at Vienna—to expose the fatuity of the classical verdict and exhibit him for what he was : the first landscape painter of his century, the acutest student of manners, and the wonderfully skilful pictorial expounder or suggester of a view of life. It is at Vienna, indeed, that Breughel's art can best be studied in all its aspects. For Vienna possesses practically all his best pictures of whatever kind. The scattered pictures at Antwerp, Brussels, Paris, Naples and elsewhere give one but the faintest notion of Breughel's powers. In the Vienna galleries are collected more than a dozen of his pictures, all belonging to his last and best period. The Tower of Babel, the great Calvary, the Numbering of the People at Bethlehem, the two Winter Landscapes and the Autumn Land-scape, the Conversion of Saint Paul, the Battle between the Israelites and the Philistines, the Marriage Feast and the Peasants' Dance—all these admirable works are here. It is on these that he must be judged.

There are four landscapes at Vienna : the Dark Day (January) and Huntsmen in the Snow (February), a November landscape (the Return of the Cattle), and the Numbering of the People at Bethlehem which in spite of its name is little

more than a landscape with figures. This last,
like the February Landscape and the Massacre of
the Innocents at Brussels, is a study of snow.
Snow scenes lent themselves particularly well to
Breughel's style of painting. For a snowy background has the effect of making all dark or
coloured objects seen against it appear in the
form of very distinct, sharp-edged silhouettes.
Breughel does in all his compositions what the
snow does in nature. All the objects in his
pictures (which are composed in a manner that
reminds one very much of the Japanese) are
paper-thin silhouettes arranged, plane after plane,
like the theatrical scenery in the depth of the stage.
Consequently in the painting of snow scenes,
where nature starts by imitating his habitual
method, he achieves an almost disquieting degree
of fundamental realism. Those hunters stepping
down over the brow of the hill towards the snowy
valley with its frozen ponds are Jack Frost himself and his crew. The crowds who move about
the white streets of Bethlehem have their being
in an absolute winter, and those ferocious troopers
looting and innocent-hunting in the midst of a
Christmas card landscape are a part of the very
army of winter, and the innocents they kill are
the young green shoots of the earth.

Breughel's method is less fundamentally compatible with the snowless landscapes of January and November. The different planes stand apart a little too flatly and distinctly. It needs a softer, bloomier kind of painting to recapture the intimate quality of such scenes as those he portrays in these two pictures. A born painter of Autumn, for example, would have fused the beasts, the men, the trees and the distant mountains into a hazier unity, melting all together, the near and the far, in the rich surface of his paint. Breughel painted too transparently and too flatly to be the perfect interpreter of such landscapes. Still, even in terms of his not entirely suitable convention he has done marvels. The Autumn Day is a thing of the most exquisite beauty. Here, as in the more sombrely dramatic January Landscape, he makes a subtle use of golds and yellows and browns, creating a sober yet luminous harmony of colours. The November Landscape is entirely placid and serene ; but in the Dark Day he has staged one of those natural dramas of the sky and earth—a conflict between light and darkness. Light breaks from under clouds along the horizon, shines up from the river in the valley that lies in the middle distance, glitters on the peaks of the mountains. The foreground, which represents the crest of a wooded hill, is dark ; and the leafless trees growing on the slopes are black against the sky. These two pictures are the most beautiful sixteenth-century landscapes of which I have any knowledge. They are intensely poetical, yet sober and not excessively picturesque or romantic. Those fearful crags and beetling precipices of which the older painters were so fond do not appear in these examples of Breughel's maturest work.

Breughel's anthropology is as delightful as his nature poetry He knew his Flemings, knew them intimately, both in their prosperity and during the miserable years of strife, of rebellion, of persecution, of war and consequent poverty which followed the advent of the Reformation in Flanders.

A Fleming himself, and so profoundly and ineradicably a Fleming that he was able to go to Italy, and, like his great countryman in the previous century, Roger van der Weyden, return without the faintest tincture of Italianism—he was perfectly qualified to be the natural historian of the Flemish folk. He exhibits them mostly in those moments of orgiastic gaiety with which they temper the laborious monotony of their daily lives : eating enormously, drinking, uncouthly dancing, indulging in that peculiarly Flemish scatological waggery. The Wedding Feast and the Peasants' Dance, both at Vienna, are superb examples of this anthropological type of painting. Nor must we forget those two curious pictures, the Battle between Carnival and Lent and the Children's Games. They too show us certain aspects of the joyous side of Flemish life. But the view is not of an individual scene, casually seized at its height and reproduced. These two pictures are systematic and encyclopaedic. In one he illustrates all children's games ; in the other all the amusements of carnival, with all the forces arrayed on the side of asceticism. In the same way he represents, in his extraordinary Tower of Babel, all the processes of building. These pictures are handbooks of their respective subjects.

Breughel's fondness for generalizing and systematizing is further illustrated in his allegorical pieces. The Triumph of Death, at the Prado, is appalling in its elaboration and completeness. The fantastic ' Dulle Griet ' at Antwerp is an almost equally elaborate triumph of evil. His illustrations to proverbs and parables belong to the same class. They show him to have been a man profoundly convinced of the reality of evil and of the horrors which this mortal life, not to mention eternity, hold in store for suffering humanity.

The world is a horrible place ; but in spite of this, or precisely because of this, men and women eat, drink and dance, Carnival tilts against Lent and triumphs, if only for a moment ; children play in the streets, people get married in the midst of gross rejoicings.

But of all Breughel's pictures the one most richly suggestive of reflection is not specifically allegorical or systematic. Christ carrying the Cross is one of his largest canvases, thronged with small figures rhythmically grouped against a wide and romantic background. The composition is simple, pleasing in itself, and seems to spring out of the subject instead of being imposed on it. So much for pure aesthetics.

Of the Crucifixion and the Carrying of the Cross there are hundreds of representations by the most admirable and diverse masters. But of all that I have ever seen this Calvary of Breughel's is the most suggestive and, dramatically, the most appalling. For all other masters have painted these dreadful scenes from within, so to speak, outwards. For them Christ is the centre, the divine hero of the tragedy ; this is the fact from which they start ; it affects and transforms all the other facts, justifying, in a sense, the horror of the drama and ranging all that surrounds the central figure in an ordered hierarchy of good and evil. Breughel, on the other hand, starts from the outside and works inwards. He represents the scene as it would have appeared to any casual spectator on the road to Golgotha on a certain spring morning in the year 33 A.D. Other artists have pretended to be angels, painting the scene with a knowledge of its significance. But Breughel resolutely remains a human onlooker. What he shows is a crowd of people walking briskly in holiday joyfulness up the slopes of a hill. On the top of the hill, which is seen in the middle distance on the right, are two crosses with thieves fastened to them, and between them a little hole in the ground in which another cross is soon to be planted. Round the crosses, on the bare hill top stands a ring of people, who have come out with their picnic baskets to look on at the free entertainment offered by the ministers of justice. Those who have already taken their stand round the crosses are the prudent ones ; in these days we should see them with camp stools and thermos flasks, six hours ahead of time, in the vanguard of the queue for a Melba night at Covent Garden. The less provident or more adventurous people are in the crowd coming up the hill with the third and greatest of the criminals

whose cross is to take the place of honour between
the other two. In their anxiety not to miss any
of the fun on the way up, they forget that they
will have to take back seats at the actual place of
execution. But it may be, of course, that they
have reserved their places, up there. At Tyburn
one could get an excellent seat in a private box for
half a crown; with the ticket in one's pocket,
one could follow the cart all the way from the
prison, arrive with the criminal and yet have a
perfect view of the performance. In these later
days, when cranky humanitarianism has so far
triumphed that hangings take place in private and
Mrs. Thompson's screams are not even allowed
to be recorded on the radio, we have to be content
with reading about executions, not with seeing
them. The impresarios who sold seats at Tyburn
have been replaced by titled newspaper proprietors
who sell juicy descriptions of Tyburn to a pro-
digiously much larger public. If people were
still hanged at Marble Arch, Lord Riddell would
be much less rich.

That eager, tremulous, lascivious interest in
blood and beastliness which in these more civilized days we can only satisfy at one remove from
reality in the pages of our newspapers, was frank-
lier indulged in Breughel's day; the naïve in-

genuous brute in man was less sophisticated, was given longer rope, and joyously barks and wags its tail round the appointed victim. Seen thus, impassively, from the outside, the tragedy does not purge or uplift ; it appals and makes desperate ; or it may even inspire a kind of gruesome mirth. The same situation may often be either tragic or comic, according as it is seen through the eyes of those who suffer or those who look on. (Shift the point of vision a little and Macbeth could be paraphrased as a roaring farce.) Breughel makes a concession to the high tragic convention by placing in the foreground of his picture a little group made up of the holy women weeping and wringing their hands. They stand quite apart from the other figures in the picture and are fundamentally out of harmony with them, being painted in the style of Roger van der Weyden. A little oasis of passionate spirituality, an island of consciousness and comprehension in the midst of the pervading stupidity and brutishness. Why Breughel put them into his picture is difficult to guess ; perhaps for the benefit of the conventionally religious, perhaps out of respect for tradition ; or perhaps he found his own creation too depressing and added this noble irrelevance to reassure himself.

Rimini was honoured, that morning, by the presence of three distinguished visitors—ourselves and the Thaumaturgical Arm of St. Francis Xavier. Divorced from the rest of the saint's remains, whose home is a jewelled tabernacle in the church of Jesus at Old Goa, the Arm, like ourselves, was making an Italian tour. But while we poor common tourists were spending money on the way, the Thaumaturgical Arm—and this was perhaps its most miraculous achievement—was raking it in. It had only to show itself through the crystal window of the reliquary in which it travelled—a skeleton arm, with a huge amethyst ring still glittering on one of the fingers of its bony hand—to command the veneration of all beholders and a copper collection, thinly interspersed with nickel and the smallest paper. The copper collection went to the foreign missions : what happened to the veneration, I do not venture to guess. It was set down, no doubt, with their offered pence, to the credit of those who felt it, in the recording angel's book.

I felt rather sorry for St. Francis Xavier's arm. The body of the saint, after translation from China to Malacca and from Malacca to India,

now reposes, as I have said, in the gaudy shrine
at Goa. After a life so extraordinarily strenuous
as was his, the great missionary deserves to rest
in peace. And so he does, most of him. But
his right arm has had to forgo its secular quiet ;
its missionary voyages are not yet over. In its
gold and crystal box it travels indefatigably
through catholic Christendom collecting pence—
'for spoiling Indian innocence,' as Mr. Matthew
Green tersely and rather tartly put it, two hundred
years ago. Poor Arm !

We found it, that morning, in the church of
San Francesco at Rimini. A crowd of adorers
filled the building and overflowed into the street
outside. The people seemed to be waiting rather
vaguely in the hope of something thaumaturgical
happening. Within the church, a long queue of
men and women shuffled slowly up into the choir
to kiss the jewelled bone-box and deposit their
soldi. Outside, among the crowd at the door of
the church, stood a number of hawkers, selling
picture postcards of the Thaumaturgical Arm and
brief but fabulous biographies of its owner. We
got into conversation with one of them, who told
us that he followed the Arm from town to town,
selling his wares wherever it stopped to show
itself. The business seemed a tolerably profit-

able one ; it enabled him, at any rate, to keep a
wife and family living in comfort at Milan.   He
showed us their photographs ; mother and children—they all looked well nourished.   But, poor
fellow ! his business kept him almost uninterruptedly away from home.   ' What does one
marry for ? ' he said as he put the photographs
back into his pocket.   ' What ? '   He sighed
and shook his head.   If only the Arm could be
induced to settle down for a little !

During the lunch hour the Arm was taken for
a drive round Rimini.   Red and yellow counter-
panes were hung out of all the windows in its
honour ; the faithful waited impatiently.   And
at last it came, driving in a very large, very noisy
and dirty old Fiat, accompanied, not, as one might
have expected, by the ecclesiastical dignitaries of
the city, but by seven or eight very secular young
men in black shirts, with frizzy hair, their trouser
pockets bulging with automatic pistols—the committee of the local fascio, no doubt.

The Arm occupied the front seat, next the
driver : the fascists lolled behind.   As the car
passed, the faithful did a very curious thing ;
mingling the gestures of reverence and applause,
they fell on their knees and clapped their hands.
The Arm was treated as though it were a com-

bination of Jackie Coogan and the Host. After lunch, it was driven rapidly away to Bologna. The vendors of sacred pictures followed as fast as the Italian trains would take them, the crowd dispersed and the church of San Francesco reverted to its habitual silence.

For this we were rather glad ; for it was not to see a fragment of St. Francis Xavier that we had come to Rimini ; it was to look at the church of St. Francis of Assisi. Sight-seeing, so long as the Arm was there, had been impossible ; its departure left us free to look round at our ease, Still, I was very glad that we had seen the peripatetic relic and its adorers in San Francesco. In this strange church which Malatesta found a Christian temple, rebuilt in pagan form and rededicated to himself, his mistress and the humanities, the scenes we had just witnessed possessed a certain piercing incongruousness that provoked— the wit of circumstances—a kind of meditative mirth. I tried to imagine what the first St. Francis would have thought of Sigismondo Malatesta, what Sigismondo thought of him and how he would have regarded the desecration of his Nietzschean temple by this posthumous visit of a bit of the second St. Francis. One can imagine a pleasant little Gobinesque or Lucianic dialogue between the four of them in the Elysian Fields, a light and airy skating over the most fearful depths of the spirit. And for those who have ears to hear there is eloquence in the dumb disputation of the stones. The Gothic arches of the interior protest against the Roman shell with which Alberti enclosed St. Francis's church ; protest against Matteo de' Pasti's pagan decorations and Malatesta's blasphemous self-exaltation ; protest, while they commend the missionary's untiring disinterestedness, against the excessive richness of his Jesuit reliquary. Grave, restrained, and intellectual, Alberti's classical façade seems to deplore the *naïveté* of the first St. Francis and the intolerant enthusiasms of the second, and, praising Malatesta's intelligence, to rebuke him for his lusts and excesses. Malatesta, meanwhile, laughs cynically at all of them. Power, pleasure and Isotta—these, he announces, through the scheme of decorations which he made Matteo de' Pasti carry out, these are the only things that matter.

The exterior of the church is entirely Alberti's Neither St. Francis nor Malatesta are allowed to disturb its solemn and harmonious beauty. Its façade is a triumphal arch, a nobler version of that arch of Augustus which spans the street at the other end of Rimini. In the colossal thickness of the southern wall, Alberti has pierced a series of deep arched niches. Recessed shadow alternates harmoniously down a long perspective with smooth sunlit stone ; and in every niche, plain and severe like the character of an early Roman in the pages of Plutarch, stands the sarcophagus of a scholar or a philosopher. There is nothing here of St. Francis's pre-lapsarian ingenuousness. Alberti is an entirely conscious adult ; he worships, but worships reason, rationally. The whole building is a hymn to intellectual beauty, an exaltation of reason as the only source of human greatness. Its form is Roman ; for Rome was the retrospective Utopia in which such men as Alberti, from the time of the Renaissance down to a much later date, saw the fulfilment of their ideals. The Roman myth dies hard, the Greek harder still ; there are certain victims of a classical education who still regard the Republic as the home of all virtues and see in Periclean Athens the unique repository of human intelligence.

Malatesta would have got a better personal apotheosis if he had lived in a later century. Alberti was too severe and stoical an artist to condescend to mere theatrical grandiosity. Nor, indeed, was the art of being grandiose really understood till the seventeenth century, the age of baroque, of kingly and clerical display. The hard-working missionary, whose arm we had seen that morning in Malatesta's temple, reposes at Goa in the sort of surroundings that would be perfectly suitable in a tyrant's self-raised shrine. Alberti's monument, on the contrary, is a tribute to intellectual greatness. As a memorial to a particularly cunning and murderous ruffian it is absurd.

In the interior of the church, it is true, Malatesta had things all his own way. Alberti was not there to interfere in his scheme of decoration, so that Sigismondo was able to dictate to Matteo de' Pasti and his colleagues all the themes of their carving. The interior is consequently one vast personal tribute to Malatesta and Isotta, with an occasional good word in favour of the pagan gods, of literature, art and science. The too expressive theatrical gesture of the baroque architects and decorators had not yet been invented ; Sigismondo's vulgar tyranny is consequently celebrated in the most perfect taste and in terms of a delicate and learned fantasy. Sigismondo got better than his deserts ; he deserved Borromini, the Cavaliere Arpino and a tenth-rate imitator of Bernini. What he actually got, owing to the accident of his date, was Matteo de' Pasti, Piero della Francesca and Leon Battista Alberti.

Alberti's share in the monument, then, is a kind of hymn to intellectual beauty, a paean in praise of civilization, couched in the language of Rome—but freely and not pedantically employed, as the philosophers and the poets of the age employed the Latin idiom. To my mind, he was almost the noblest Roman of them all. The exterior of San Francesco at Rimini, the interior of Sant' Andrea at Mantua (sadly daubed about by later decorators and with Juvara's absurd high-drummed cupola in the midst instead of the saucer dome designed by Alberti himself) are as fine as anything in the whole range of renaissance architecture. What renders them the more remarkable is that they were without precedent, in his age. Alberti was one of the re-inventors of the style. Of his particular Roman manner, indeed (the manner which became the current idiom of the later renaissance) he was the sole re-discoverer. The other early renaissance manner, based, like Alberti's, on the classics—the manner of Brunelleschi—was doomed, so far at any rate as ecclesiastical architecture was concerned, to extinction. Sant' Andrea at Mantua is the model from which the typical churches of the

later renaissance were imitated, not Brunelleschi's
Florentine San Lorenzo or Santo Spirito.

A comparison between these nearly contemporary architects—Brunelleschi was born some
twenty-five years before Alberti—is extremely interesting and instructive. Both were enthusiastic
students of the antique, both knew their Rome,
both employed in their buildings the characteristic
elements of classical architecture. And yet it
would be difficult to discover two architects whose
work is more completely dissimilar. Compare
the interiors of Brunelleschi's two Florentine
churches with that of Alberti's Sant' Andrea.
Brunelleschi's churches are divided into a nave
and aisles by rows of tall slender pillars supporting
round arches. The details are classical and so
correct that they might have been executed by
Roman workmen. But the general design is not
Roman, but Romanesque. His churches are
simply more spidery versions of eleventh-century
basilicas, with 'purer' details. All is airiness
and lightness ; there is even a certain air of in-
security about these church interiors, so slender
are the pillars, so much free space is to be seen.

What a contrast with Alberti's great church !
It is built in the form of a Latin cross, with a
single nave and side chapels. The nave is barrel-

vaulted ; over the crossing is a dome (Juvara's, unfortunately, not Alberti's) ; the altar is placed in an apse. The chapels open on to the central nave by tall, and proportionately wide, round-headed arches. Between each of the chapels is a gigantic pier of masonry, as wide as the arches which they separate. A small door is pierced in each of these piers, giving access to subsidiary chapels hollowed out of their mass. But the doors are inconspicuous and the general effect is one of void and solid equally alternating. Alberti's is essentially the architecture of masses, Brunelleschi's of lines. Even to the enormous dome of Santa Maria del Fiore Brunelleschi contrives to impart an extraordinary lightness, as of lines with voids between them. The huge mass hangs aerially from its eight ribs of marble. A miracle is effortlessly consummated before our eyes. But a dome, however light you make it, is essentially an affair of masses. In designing his cupola for Santa Maria del Fiore Brunelleschi found the plastic view of things imposed upon him. That is why, it may be, the dome is so incomparably the finest thing he ever made. He was not permitted by the nature of the architectural problem to be solved to give free play to his passion for lightness and the fine line. He was

dealing here with masses ; it could not be escaped.
The result was that, treating the mass of the dome
as far as was possible in terms of light, strong, leaping lines, he contrived to impart to his work an
elegance and an aerial strength such as have never
been equalled in any other dome.   The rest of
Brunelleschi's work, however charming and
graceful, is, to my mind at any rate, far less
satisfying, precisely because it is so definitely an
affair of lines.   Brunelleschi studied the architecture of the Romans ; but he took from it only
its details.   What was essential in it—its majestic
massiveness—did not appeal to him.   He preferred, in all his church designs, to refine and
refine on the work of the romanesque architects,
until at last he arrived at a slender and precarious
elegance that was all vacuum and outline.

Alberti, on the other hand, took from the
Romans their fundamental conception of an
architecture of masses and developed it, with
refinements, for modern, Christian uses.   To my
mind, he was the better and truer architect of the
two.   For I personally like massiveness and an
air of solidity.   Others, I know, prefer lines and
lightness and would put the interior of San
Lorenzo above that of Sant' Andrea, the Pazzi
chapel above San Francesco at Rimini.   We shall

never be reconciled. All who practise the visual arts and, presumably, all who appreciate them must have some kind of feeling for form as such. But not all are interested in the same kind of forms. The lovers of pure line and the lovers of mass stand at opposite ends of an aesthetic scale. The aesthetic passion of one artist, or one art lover, is solidity ; another is moved only by linear arabesques on a flat surface. Those formal passions may be misplaced. Painters may be led by their excessive love of three-dimensional solidity quite beyond the field of painting ; Michelangelo is an obvious example. Sculptors with too great a fondness for mere linear effect cease to be sculptors, and their work is no more than a flat decoration in stone or metal, meant to be seen from only one point of view and having no depth ; the famous Diana attributed to Goujon (but probably by Benvenuto Cellini) is one of these statues conceived in the flat. Just as painters must not be too fond of solidity, nor sculptors too much attached to flatness, so, it seems to me, no architect should be too exclusively interested in lines. Architecture in the hands of a linear enthusiast takes on the too slender, spidery elegance of Brunelleschi's work.

The psycho-analysts, who trace all interest in

art back to an infantile love of excrement, would doubtless offer some simple faecal explanation for the varieties in our aesthetic passions. One man loves masses, another lines : the explanation in terms of coprophily is so obvious that I may be excused from giving it here. I will content myself by quoting from the works of Dr. Ernest Jones, the reason why the worship of form should come to be connected in so many cases with the worship of a moral ideal ; in a word, why art is so often religious. ' Religion,' says Dr. Jones, ' has always used art in one form or another, and must do so, for the reason that incestuous desires invariably construct their phantasies out of the material provided by the unconscious memory of infantile coprophilic interests ; that is the inner meaning of the phrase, " Art is the handmaid of Religion." ' Illuminating and beautiful words ! It is a pity they were not written thirty years ago. I should have liked to read Tolstoy's comments in *What is Art ?* on this last and best of the aesthetic theories.

CONXOLUS

To know what everybody else knows—that Virgil, for example, wrote the *Aeneid*, or that the sum of the angles of a triangle is equal to two right angles—is rather boring and undistinguished. If you want to acquire a reputation for learning at a cheap rate, it is best to ignore the dull and stupid knowledge which is everybody's possession and concentrate on something odd and out of the way. Instead of quoting Virgil quote Sidonius Apollinaris, and express loudly your contempt of those who prefer the court poet of Augustus to the panegyrist of Avitus, Majorianus and Anthemius. When the conversation turns on *Jane Eyre* or *Wuthering Heights* (which of course you have not read) say you infinitely prefer *The Tenant of Wildfell Hall*. When Donne is praised, pooh-pooh him and tell the praiser that he should read Gongora. At the mention of Raphael, make as though to vomit outright (though you have never been inside the Vatican); the Raphael Mengses at Petersburg, you will say, are the only tolerable paintings. In this way you will get the reputation of a person of profound learning and the most exquisite taste. Whereas, if you give proof of knowing your

Dickens, of having read the Bible, the English classics, Euclid and Horace, nobody will think anything of you at all. You will be just like everybody else.

The extreme inadequacy of my education has often led me, in the course of my journalistic career, to adopt these tactics. I have written airily of the remote and odd in order to conceal my ignorance of the near and the classical. The profession of a literary journalist is not one that greatly encourages honesty. Everything conspires to make him a charlatan. He has no leisure to read regularly or with purpose ; at the same time reviewing makes him acquainted with a mass of fragmentary and miscellaneous information. He would be a prodigy of intellectual integrity if he did not reproduce it in his own articles, casually and with confidence, as though each queer item were an outlying promontory of the vast continent of his universal knowledge. Moreover the necessity under which he labours of always being readable tempts him at all costs to be original and unusual. Is it to be wondered at if, knowing five lines each of Virgil and Apollinaris, he prefers to quote the latter ? Or if, knowing none of Virgil, he turns his ignorance into a critical virtue and lets it be understood that

the best minds have now gone on from Maro to
Sidonius ?

In the monastery of Subiaco, which lies in that
remote back of beyond behind Tivoli, there are,
among many other things of beauty and historical
interest, a number of frescoes by a thirteenth-
century master, unknown except as the author of
these works, called Conxolus. The name is
superb and could not be improved. Majestic
and at the same time slightly grotesque, uncommon (indeed, for all I know, unique) and
easily memorable, it is a name which seems by
right to belong to a great man. Conxolus : at
the sound of those rich syllables the cultured
person has a vague uncomfortable feeling that he
ought to know what they connote. Is it a
battle ? or scholastic philosophy ? or a heresy ?
or what ? Learning, after a moment's agonizing
suspense (during which he is uncertain whether
his interlocutor will let out the secret or force him
to confess his ignorance) that Conxolus was a
painter, the cultured person confidently plunges.
' Such a *mar*vellous artist ! ' he rapturously
exclaims.

The old journalistic Adam is not quite dead
within me, and I know my cultured society.
The temptation was strong. I would preach

Conxolus to a benighted world and, exalting him
as an artist, exalt myself at the same time as an art
critic.   And how cheaply !   For the price of
three gallons of petrol, ten francs of post-cards and
tips, and an excellent lunch, with trout, at Tivoli,
I should have made myself completely master of
my subject and established my *Kunstforscher's*
reputation.   No tiresome journeys to far away
galleries in search of the master's minor works,
no laborious reading of German monographs.
Just this one extremely agreeable trip to the upper
Anio, this forty minutes' walk uphill, this little
trot round Saint Benedict's first hermitage—and
that was all.   I would go back to London, I
would write some articles, or even a little book,
with handsome reproductions, about the master.
And when, in cultured society, people talked of
Duccio or Simone Martini, I should smile from
the height of my superiority.   'They are all very
well, no doubt.   But when one has seen Conxolus.'   And I should go on talking of his tactile
and olfactory values, his magistral treatment of
the fourth dimension, his exquisitely subtle use
of *repoussoirs* and that extraordinary mastery of
colour which enabled him to paint all the flesh in
his pictures in two tones of ochre, impure purple
and goose-turd green.   And my auditors (terri-

fied, as all the frequenters of cultured society always are, of being left behind in the intellectual race), would listen with grave avidity. And they would leave me, triumphantly conscious that they had scored a point over their rivals, that they had entered a new swim from which all but the extremely select were excluded, that their minds were dressed in a fashion that came straight from Paris (for of course I should give them to understand that Derain and Matisse entirely agreed with me) ; and from that day forth the name of Conxolus, and with it my name, would begin to reverberate, *crescendo*, with an ever-growing rumour of admiration, in all the best drawing-rooms, from Euston to the World's End.

The temptation was strong ; but I wrestled with it heroically and at last had the mastery. I decided that I would not pervert the truth for the sake of any reputation, however flattering, for critical insight and discrimination. For the truth, alas, is that our unique and high-sounding Conxolus is an entirely negligible painter. Competent and well-trained ; but no more. His principal merit consists in the fact that he lived in the thirteenth century and worked in the characteristic style of his period. He painted in the decadent Byzantine manner which we, arguing

backwards from sixteenth-century Florence instead of forwards from sixth-century Ravenna,
miscall 'primitive.' It is in this, I repeat, that
his principal merit consists—at any rate for us.
For a century ago his primitiveness would only
have aroused derision and pity. We have changed
all that nowadays ; and so thoroughly that there
are many young people who, in their anxiety not
to be thought old-fashioned, regard all pictures
bearing a close resemblance to their subjects as
highly suspicious and, unless guaranteed chemic-
ally pure by some recognized aesthetic authority,
a priori ridiculous. To these ascetics all natural
beauty, when reproduced by art, is damnable. A
beautiful woman accurately painted is 'chocolate
boxy' ; a beautiful landscape mere poetry. If a
work of art is obviously charming, if it moves at
first sight, then, according to these people, it must
also necessarily be bad. This doctrine applied to
music has led to the exaltation of Bach, even Bach
in his most mechanical and soulless moments, at
the expense of Beethoven. It has led to the dry
'classical' way of playing Mozart, who is supposed to be unemotional because he is not vulgarly
emotional, like Wagner. It has led to steam
organ-like performances of Handel and senseless
bellowings of Palestrina. And the absurd young,

in reaction against the sentimentalities and lach-
rymose idealisms which they imagine to have
characterized the later Victorian age, being left
absolutely unmoved by these performances, have
for that very reason applauded them as in the
highest degree artistic.   It is the same in painting.
The muddier the colours, the more distorted the
figures, the higher the art.   There are hundreds
of young painters who dare not paint realistically
and charmingly, even if they could, for fear of
losing the esteem of the young connoisseurs who
are their patrons.   True, good painters paint well
and express all they have to say whatever convention they may use ; and indifferent painters paint
indifferently in all circumstances.   It ought,
therefore, to give us no concern whatever if indifferent young painters do prefer distortion and
muddy colouring to gaiety, realism and charm.
It does not seriously matter how they paint.   At
the same time the world did get a certain amount
of entertainment out of its indifferent painters in
the past, when they did their best to imitate nature
and tell stories.   It got faithful copies of beautiful
objects, it got documents and pictorial notes, it
got amusing anecdotes and comments on life.
These things might not be great pictures ; but
they were at any rate worth something, for they

had an other than aesthetic value. Aiming as he does at some mythical ideal of pure aestheticism, to which all but form is sacrificed, the young talentless painter of the present time gives us nothing but boredom. For his pictures are not good pictures, and they do not make amends for their badness by reminding us of pleasing objects ; they have not even the merit of being documents or comments, they do not even tell a story. In a word they have nothing to recommend them. From being an entertainer, the second-rate artist (if he happens also to be ' advanced ') has become an intolerable bore.

The young's mistrust of realism does not apply only to contemporary art ; it is also retrospective. Of two equally untalented artists of the past youth unhesitatingly prefers the man who is least realistic, most ' primitive.' Conxolus is admired above his seventeenth-century counterpart, simply because his figures remind one of nothing that is charming in nature, because he is innocent of light and shade, because the composition is rigidly symmetrical and because the emotional content of his ardently Christian pictures has, for us, completely evaporated, leaving nothing that can evoke in our bosoms the slightest sentiment of any kind, with the single exception of those famous

aesthetic emotions which the young so studiously
cultivate.

True, the convention in which the seventeenth-century Italian painters worked was an
intolerable one. The wild gesticulations with
which they filled their pictures, in the hope of
artificially creating an atmosphere of passion, is
fundamentally ludicrous. The baroque style and
the kindred romantic style are the two styles best
fitted in the nature of things for the expression of
comedy. Aristophanes, Rabelais, Nashe, Balzac,
Dickens, Rowlandson, Goya, Doré, Daumier and
the nameless makers of grotesques all over the
world and at every period—all practitioners of
pure comedy, whether in literature or in art—
have employed an extravagant, baroque, romantic
style. Naturally ; for pure comedy it is essentially extravagant and enormous. Except in the
hands of prodigious men of genius (such as Mar-
lowe and Shakespeare, Michelangelo and Rembrandt) this style, when used for serious purposes,
is ludicrous. Almost all baroque art and almost
all the kindred romantic art of a later epoch are
grotesque because the artists (not of the first order)
are trying to express something tragic in terms of a
style essentially comic. In this respect the works
of the 'primitives'—even of the second-rate

primitives—are really preferable to the works of their *seicento* descendants. For in their pictures there is no fundamental incongruity between the style and subject. But this is a negative quality ; second-rate primitives are decent but they are extraordinarily dull. The work of the later realists may be vulgar and absurd as a whole ; but it is redeemed, very often, by the charm of its details. You can find, in the pictures of second-rate artists of the seventeenth century, charming landscapes, interesting physiognomies, studies of curious effects of light and shade—things which do nothing, it is true, to redeem these works, viewed as wholes, from badness, but are nevertheless agreeable and interesting in themselves. In the Conxoluses of an earlier epoch the work as a whole is respectable ; but its dullness is not relieved by any curious or delightful details. By their absurdly ascetic distrust of the obviously delightful, the young have deprived themselves of a great deal of pleasure. They bore themselves by second-rate Conxoluses when they might amuse themselves by equally second-rate Fetis and Caravaggios and Rosa da Tivolis and Carpionis and Guercinos and Luca Giordanos and all the rest of them. If one must look at second-rate pictures at all —and there are so few good pictures that one inevitably must—it is surely more reasonable to look at those which give one something (even though the plums be embedded in a suet of horror) than those which give one absolutely nothing at all.

THE BEST PICTURE

Borgo San Sepolcro is not very easy to get at. There is a small low-comedy railway across the hills from Arezzo. Or you can approach it up the Tiber valley from Perugia. Or, if you happen to be at Urbino, there is a motor 'bus which takes you to San Sepolcro, up and down through the Apennines, in something over seven hours. No joke, that journey, as I know by experience. But it is worth doing, though preferably in some other vehicle than the 'bus, for the sake of the Bocca Trabaria, that most beautiful of Apennine passes, between the Tiber valley and the upper valley of the Metauro. It was in the early spring that we crossed it. Our omnibus groaned and rattled slowly up a bleak northern slope, among bald rocks, withered grass and still unbudded trees. It crossed the col and suddenly, as though by a miracle, the ground was yellow with innumerable primroses, each flower a little emblem of the sun that had called it into being.

And when at last one has arrived at San Sepolcro, what is there to be seen? A little town surrounded by walls, set in a broad flat valley between hills; some fine renaissance palaces with pretty balconies of wrought iron;

a not very interesting church, and finally, the best picture in the world.

The best picture in the world is painted in fresco on the wall of a room in the town hall. Some unwittingly beneficent vandal had it covered, some time after it was painted, with a thick layer of plaster, under which it lay hidden for a century or two, to be revealed at last in a state of preservation remarkably perfect for a fresco of its date. Thanks to the vandals, the visitor who now enters the Palazzo dei Conservatori at Borgo San Sepolcro finds the stupendous Resurrection almost as Piero della Francesca left it. Its clear, yet subtly sober colours shine out from the wall with scarcely impaired freshness. Damp has blotted out nothing of the design, nor dirt obscured it. We need no imagination to help us figure forth its beauty ; it stands there before us in entire and actual splendour, the greatest picture in the world.

The greatest picture in the world. . . . You smile. The expression is ludicrous, of course. Nothing is more futile than the occupation of those connoisseurs who spend their time compiling first and second elevens of the world's best painters, eights and fours of musicians, fifteens of poets, all-star troupes of architects and so on.

Nothing is so futile because there are a great many kinds of merit and an infinite variety of human beings. Is Fra Angelico a better artist than Rubens? Such questions, you insist, are meaningless. It is all a matter of personal taste. And up to a point this is true. But there does exist, none the less, an absolute standard of artistic merit. And it is a standard which is in the last resort a moral one. Whether a work of art is good or bad depends entirely on the quality of the character which expresses itself in the work. Not that all virtuous men are good artists, nor all artists conventionally virtuous. Longfellow was a bad poet, while Beethoven's dealings with his publishers were frankly dishonourable. But one can be dishonourable towards one's publishers and yet preserve the kind of virtue that is necessary to a good artist. That virtue is the virtue of integrity, of honesty towards oneself. Bad art is of two sorts : that which is merely dull, stupid and incompetent, the negatively bad ; and the positively bad, which is a lie and a sham. Very often the lie is so well told that almost every one is taken in by it—for a time. In the end, however, lies are always found out. Fashion changes, the public learns to look with a different focus and, where a little while ago it saw an admirable work which actually moved its emotions, it now sees a sham. In the history of the arts we find innumerable shams of this kind, once taken as genuine, now seen to be false. The very names of most of them are now forgotten. Still, a dim rumour that Ossian once was read, that Bulwer was thought a great novelist and 'Festus' Bailey a mighty poet still faintly reverberates. Their counterparts are busily earning praise and money at the present day. I often wonder if I am one of them. It is impossible to know. For one can be an artistic swindler without meaning to cheat and in the teeth of the most ardent desire to be honest.

Sometimes the charlatan is also a first-rate man of genius and then you have such strange artists as Wagner and Bernini, who can turn what is false and theatrical into something almost sublime.

That it is difficult to tell the genuine from the sham is proved by the fact that enormous numbers of people have made mistakes and continue to make them. Genuineness, as I have said, always triumphs in the long run. But at any given moment the majority of people, if they do not actually prefer the sham to the real, at least like it as much, paying an indiscriminate homage to both.

And now, after this little digression we can return to San Sepolcro and the greatest picture in the world. Great it is, absolutely great, because the man who painted it was genuinely noble as well as talented. And to me personally the most moving of pictures, because its author possessed almost more than any other painter those qualities of character which I most admire and because his purely aesthetic preoccupations are of a kind which I am by nature best fitted to understand. A natural, spontaneous, and unpretentious grandeur—this is the leading quality of all Piero's work. He is majestic without being at all strained, theatrical or hysterical—as Handel is majestic, not as Wagner. He achieves grandeur naturally with every gesture he makes, never consciously strains after it. Like Alberti, with whose architecture, as I hope to show, his painting has certain affinities, Piero seems to have been inspired by what I may call the religion of Plutarch's *Lives*—which is not Christianity, but a worship of what is admirable in man. Even his technically religious pictures are paeans in praise of human dignity. And he is everywhere intellectual.

With the drama of life and religion he is very little concerned. His battle pictures at Arezzo are not dramatic compositions in spite of the many dramatic incidents they contain. All the turmoil, all the emotions of the scenes have been digested by the mind into a grave intellectual whole. It is as though Bach had written the 1812 Overture. Nor are the two superb pictures in the National Gallery—the Nativity and the Baptism—distinguished for any particular sympathy with the religious or emotional significance of the events portrayed. In the extraordinary Flagellation at Urbino, the nominal subject of the picture recedes into the background on the left-hand side of the panel, where it serves to balance the three mysterious figures standing aloof in the right foreground. We seem to have nothing here but an experiment in composition, but an experiment so strange and so startlingly successful that we do not regret the absence of dramatic significance and are entirely satisfied. The Resurrection at San Sepolcro is more dramatic. Piero has made the simple triangular composition symbolic of the subject. The base of the triangle is formed by the sepulchre ; and the soldiers sleeping round it are made to indicate by their position the upward jet of the two sides, which meet at the apex in the face of the risen Christ, who is standing, a banner in his right hand, his left foot already raised and planted on the brim of the sepulchre, preparing to set out into the world. No geometrical arrangement could have been more simple or more apt. But the being who rises before our eyes from the tomb is more like a Plutarchian hero than the Christ of conventional religion. The body is perfectly developed, like that of a Greek athlete ; so formidably strong that the wound in its muscular flank seems somehow an irrelevance. The face is stern and pensive, the eyes cold. The whole figure is expressive of physical and intellectual power. It is the resurrection of the classical ideal, incredibly much grander and more beautiful than the classical reality, from the tomb where it had lain so many hundred years.

Aesthetically, Piero's work has this resemblance to Alberti's : that it too is essentially an affair of masses. What Alberti is to Brunelleschi, Piero della Francesca is to his contemporary, Botticelli. Botticelli was fundamentally a draughtsman, a maker of supple and resilient lines, thinking in terms of arabesques inscribed on the flat. Piero, on the contrary, has a passion for solidity as such. There is something in all his works that reminds one constantly of Egyptian sculpture. Piero has that Egyptian love of the smooth rounded surface that is the external symbol and expression of a mass. The faces of his personages look as though they were carved out of some very hard rock into which it had been impossible to engrave the details of a human physiognomy—the hollows, the lines and wrinkles of real life. They are ideal, like the faces of Egyptian gods and princes, surface meeting and marrying with curved unbroken surface in an almost geometrical fashion. Look, for example, at the faces of the women in Piero's fresco at Arezzo : 'The Queen of Sheba recognizing the Holy Tree.' They are all of one peculiar cast : the foreheads are high, rounded and smooth ; the necks are like cylinders of polished ivory ; from the midst of the concave sockets the eyelids swell out in one uninterrupted curve into convexity ; the cheeks are unbrokenly smooth and the subtle curvature of their surfaces is indicated by a very delicate chiaroscuro which suggests more powerfully the solidity and mass of the flesh than the most spectacular Caravaggioesque light and shade could do.

Piero's passion for solidity betrays itself no less strikingly in his handling of the dresses and drapery of his figures. It is noticeable, for example, that wherever the subject permits, he makes his personages appear in curious head-dresses that remind one by their solid geometrical qualities of those oddly-shaped ceremonial hats or tiaras worn by the statues of Egyptian kings. Among the frescoes at Arezzo are several which illustrate this peculiarity. In that representing Heraclius restoring the True Cross to Jerusalem, all the ecclesiastical dignitaries are wearing enormously high head-dresses, conical, trumpet-shaped, even rectangular. They are painted very smoothly with, it is obvious, a profound relish for their solidity. One or two similar head-dresses, with many varieties of wonderfully rounded helmets, are lovingly represented in the battle-pieces in the same place. The Duke of Urbino, in the well-known portrait at the Uffizi, is wearing a red cloth cap whose shape is somewhat like that of the 'Brodrick' of the modern English soldier, but without the peak—a cylinder fitting round the head, topped by a projecting disk as the crown. Its smoothness and the roundness of its surfaces are emphasized in the picture. Nor does Piero neglect the veils of his female figures. Though transparent and of lawn, they hang round the heads of his women in stiff folds, as though they were made of steel. Among clothes he has a special fondness for pleated bodices and tunics. The bulge and recession of the pleated

stuff fascinates him and he likes to trace the way
in which the fluted folds follow the curve of the
body beneath. To drapery he gives, as we might
expect, a particular weight and richness. Perhaps his most exquisite handling of drapery is to
be seen in the altar-piece of the Madonna della
Misericordia, which now hangs near the Resurrection in the town hall at San Sepolcro. The
central figure in this picture, which is one of the
earliest of Piero's extant works, represents the
Virgin, standing, and stretching out her arms, so
as to cover two groups of suppliants on either side
with the folds of her heavy blue mantle. The
mantle and the Virgin's dress hang in simple
perpendicular folds, like the flutings on the robe
of the archaic bronze charioteer at the Louvre.
Piero has painted these alternately convex and
concave surfaces with a peculiar gusto.

It is not my intention to write a treatise on
Piero della Francesca ; that has been done sufficiently often and sufficiently badly to make it
unnecessary for me to bury that consummate
artist any deeper under layers of muddy comment.
All I have meant to do in this place is to give the
reasons why I like his works and my justifications
for calling the Resurrection the greatest picture in
the world. I am attracted to his character by his

intellectual power ; by his capacity for unaffect-
edly making the grand and noble gesture ; by his
pride in whatever is splendid in humanity.   And
in the artist I find peculiarly sympathetic the lover
of solidity, the painter of smooth curving surfaces,
the composer who builds with masses.   For myself I prefer him to Botticelli, so much so indeed,
that if it were necessary to sacrifice all Botticelli's
works in order to save the Resurrection, the
Nativity, the Madonna della Misericordia and the
Arezzo frescoes, I should unhesitatingly commit
the Primavera and all the rest of them to the
flames.   It is unfortunate for Piero's reputation
that his works should be comparatively few and
in most cases rather difficult of access.   With the
exception of the Nativity and Baptism at the
National Gallery, all the really important works
of Piero are at Arezzo, San Sepolcro and Urbino.
The portraits of the Duke and Duchess of Urbino
with their respective triumphs, in the Uffizi, are
charming and exceedingly ' amusing ' ; but they
do not represent Piero at his best.   The altar-
piece at Perugia and the Madonna with saints and
donor at Milan are neither of them first-rate.
The St. Jerome at Venice is goodish ; so too is
the damaged fresco of the Malatesta, at Rimini.
The Louvre possesses nothing and Germany can

only boast of a study of architecture, inferior to that at Urbino. Anybody, therefore, who wants to know Piero, must go from London to Arezzo, San Sepolcro and Urbino. Now Arezzo is a boring sort of town, and so ungrateful to its distinguished sons that there is no monument within its walls to the divine Aretino. I deplore Arezzo ; but to Arezzo, nevertheless, you must go to see Piero's most considerable works. From Arezzo you must make your way to San Sepolcro, where the inn is only just tolerable, and to which the means of communication are so bad that, unless you come in your own car, you are fairly compelled to stay there. And from San Sepolcro you must travel by 'bus for seven hours across the Apennines to Urbino. Here, it is true, you have not only two admirable Pieros (the Flagellation and an architectural scene), but the most exquisite palace in Italy and very nearly a good hotel. Even on the most wearily reluctant tourist Urbino imposes itself ; there is no escaping it ; it must be seen. But in the case of Arezzo and San Sepolcro there is no such moral compulsion. Few tourists, in consequence, take the trouble to visit them.

If the principal works of Piero were to be seen in Florence, and those of Botticelli at San Sepolcro

I do not doubt that the public estimation of these two masters would be reversed. Artistic English spinsters would stand in rapturous contemplation before the story of the True Cross, instead of before the Primavera. Raptures depend largely upon the stars in Baedeker, and the stars are more freely distributed to works of art in accessible towns than to those in the inaccessible. If the Arena chapel were in the mountains of Calabria, instead of at Padua, we should all have heard a good deal less of Giotto.

But enough. The shade of Conxolus rises up to remind me that I am running into the error of those who measure merit by a scale of oddness and rarity.

'A LITTLE learning,' said Pope, 'is a dangerous thing.' And who, indeed, should have known its dangers more intimately than the man who had undertaken to translate Homer without (for all practical purposes) knowing a word of Greek? 'Drink deep'—the exhortation, you feel, comes from the translator's very heart—'or taste not the Pierian spring.'

Drink deep. The advice is good, provided always that the liquor be a sound one. But is the Pierian spring sound? That is the question. Not all medicinal waters are good for every drinker. People who can profitably drink deep of Carlsbad or Montecatini may die of a surfeit of Bath. Similarly the Pierian spring is not for everybody. The philosopher and the man of science may drink of it as deeply as they like and it will do them nothing but good. To the poet it can certainly do no harm; his native woodnotes are enriched by a little learning. The politician would do well to drink of this spring more often and more copiously than he actually does. The man of business may find profit in the draught, while the dilettante drinks for mere pleasure. But there is at least one class of men to whom the Pierian spring seems to be almost fatal. On no account should the artist be allowed to drink of it.

Two centuries have passed since Pope warned his readers against the dangers of a little learning. The history of those two centuries, and especially of the last fifty years, has proved that, so far as the artist is concerned, much learning is quite as dangerous as little learning. It is, in fact, a great deal more dangerous.

I can best explain what happens when artists drink deep of the Pierian spring by describing a kind of Arts and Crafts exhibition which I happened to see, a summer or two since, in Munich. It was a huge affair. Furniture, jewellery, ceramics, textiles—every kind of applied art was copiously represented. And all the exhibits were German. All German—and yet these pots and pans, these chairs and tables, these weavings, paintings, carvings, forgings spoke a hundred languages besides the native Teuton. Aryan, Mongolian, Semitic, Bantu, Polynesian, Maya— the stocks and stones of Munich were fluent in all the tongues. Here, for example, stood a Mexican pot, decorated with Moorish arabesques; here a statuette that was sixth-century Greek, subtly mingled with Benin. Here was a Black

Forest peasant's table standing on Egyptian legs ; here a crucifix that might have been carved by a T'ang artist who happened to have spent a year in Italy as the pupil of Bernini. Goat, woman, lion and gryphon—here were chimaeras and empusas at every turn. And none of them (that was the real horror, for success justifies every-thing) none of them were good.

Germany, it is true, is the country where the dangers of too much learning have made them-selves most apparent. It is the country that has drunk most deeply of the Pierian spring. For the last fifty years German publishers have brought out six illustrated monographs to every one produced in France, and a dozen at least to every one that we have published in England. With untiring industry and an enthusiasm which nothing—not the War, not even the Peace—has been able to damp, the Germans have photo-graphed the artistic remains of every people that has ever flourished on the face of the earth. And they have published these photographs, with learned prefaces, in little books, which they sold, once upon a time, for a mark apiece, and which even now do not cost more than, shall we say, fif-teen or twenty thousand millions. The Germans know more about the artistic styles of the past than any other people in the world—and their own art, to-day, is about as hopelessly dreary as any national art could well be. Its badness is, in mathematical terms, a function of its learnedness.

What has happened in Germany has happened, though to a slightly less marked degree, in every country of the world. We all know too much, and our knowledge prevents us—unless we happen to be artists of exceptional independence and talent—from doing good work.

Up till quite recently no European artist knew, or thought it worth while to know, anything about any forms of art except those which had been current in his own continent. And even of those he knew precious little. A sixteenth-century sculptor, for example, knew something about Greek carving—or something, at any rate, about Roman copies of carvings belonging to a certain period of Greek art. But of the works which the sculptors of the Gothic past had produced, even in his own country, he knew very little ; and what he knew, he was disposed to deride as being merely barbarous. There were no photographs then ; there were even very few engravings. The renaissance sculptor worked in an almost total ignorance of what had been done by other sculptors, at other periods or in countries other than his own. The result was that he was able to concentrate on the one convention that seemed to him good—the classical— and work away at it undisturbed, until he had developed all its potential resources.

The case of architecture is still more remarkable. For three hundred years the classical orders reigned supreme in Europe. Gothic was forgotten and despised. Nobody knew anything of any other styles. Generation after generation of architects worked away uninterruptedly in terms of this one convention. And what an astonishing variety of achievements they were able to get out of it ! Using the same elementary classical units, successive generations produced a series of absolutely original and dissimilar works. Brunelleschi, Alberti, Michelangelo, Palladio, Bernini, Pietro da Cortona, Christopher Wren, Adam, Nash— all these architects worked in the same classical convention, making it yield a series of distinctive masterpieces, each utterly unlike the other.

These were all men of genius who would have done great things in any circumstances. What is still more striking is the achievement of the minor artists. During all this long period the work of even a journeyman had qualities which we look for in vain among the lesser artists of the present time. It was the absence of distracting knowledge that made possible this high level of achievement among the less talented men. There was for them only one possible convention. They concentrated their whole mind on getting the best they possibly could out of it.

How different is the present state of affairs ! The artist of to-day knows, and has been taught to appreciate, the artistic conventions of every people that has ever existed. For him, there is no single right convention ; there are a thousand conventions, which can all claim his respect because men have produced fine works in terms of all of them. Gone is the blessed ignorance, vanished the healthy contempt for all but one tradition. There is no tradition now, or there are a hundred traditions—it comes to the same thing. The artist's knowledge tends to distract him, to dissipate his energies. Instead of spending his whole life systematically exploiting one convention, he moves restlessly among all the known styles, undecided which to work in, borrowing hints from each.

But in art there are no short cuts to successful achievement. You cannot acquire in half an hour the secrets of a style which it has taken the work of generations to refine to its perfection. In half an hour, it is true, you can learn what are the most striking superficial characteristics of the style ; you can learn to caricature it. That is all. To understand a style you must give yourself up to it ; you must live, so to speak, inside it ; you must concentrate and steadily labour.

But concentration is precisely the thing which excessive knowledge tends to render impossible —for all, at any rate, but the most individually gifted, the most strong-minded of artists. They, it is true, can be left to look after themselves. Whatever their mental and physical environment, they will be themselves. Knowledge has had its most disastrous effects on the minor men, on the rank and file. These, in another century, would have worked away undistracted, trying to get the best out of a single convention—trying and, what is more, generally succeeding to the very limit of their natural capacities. Their descendants are trying to get the best out of fifty different conventions at once. With what results Munich most hideously shows. And not only Munich, but Paris too, London, New York, the whole knowledge-ridden world.

Still, the knowledge exists and is easily available. There is no destroying or concealing it.

There can be no recapture of the old ignorance which allowed the artists of the past to go on working in one style for years, for centuries even, at a time.   Knowledge has brought with it rest-lessness, uncertainty and the possibility of rapid and incessant change in the conventions of art. How many styles have come and gone during the last seventy years !   Pre-Raphaelitism, impres-sionism, art nouveau, futurism, post-impression-ism, cubism, expressionism.   It would have taken the Egyptians a hundred centuries to run through such a fortune of styles.   To-day, we invent a new convention—or, more often, resuscitate a combination of old conventions out of the past— exploit it, and throw it away, all in the space of five years.   The fixity of the old traditions, the sure refinement of taste, born of ignorance and intolerant fastidiousness, have gone.   Will they ever return ?   In time, no doubt, the artists will have inured themselves to the poison of the Pierian spring.   The immense mass of know-ledge which, in our minds, is still crude, will gradually be digested.   When that has happened, some sort of fixity—or rather some slow and steady motion, for in life there is no fixity—will have been achieved.   Meanwhile, we must be content to live in an age of dissipated energies, of

experiment and pastiche, of restlessness and hopeless uncertainty.

The vast increase in our knowledge of art
history has affected not only the artists themselves,
but all those who take an interest in the arts.
For *tout savoir est tout pardonner* ; we have
learned to appreciate and see the best in every
style. To Voltaire and Dr. Johnson even Gothic
art seemed a barbarism. What would they have
said if we had asked them to admire the plastic
beauties of a Polynesian statue, or the painting of
an animal by an artist who lived millenniums
before the dawn of history ? Knowledge has
enabled us to sympathize with unfamiliar points
of view, to appreciate artistic conventions devised
by people utterly unlike ourselves. All this, no
doubt, is a very good thing. But our sympathy
is so vast and we are so much afraid of showing
ourselves intolerant towards the things we ought
to like, that we have begun to love in our all-
embracing way not merely the highest, in whatever convention, when we see it, but the lowest
too.

We are not content with appreciating the good
things which our ancestors condemned. Appetite
grows with what it feeds on. The good is not
enough to satisfy our hungry appreciation ; we

must swallow the bad as well. To justify ourselves in this appreciation of what is bad, we have created a whole series of new aesthetic values. The process which began some time ago has gone on with ever-increasing speed and thoroughness, till there is now almost nothing, however bad, from which we cannot derive pleasure.

Historically, I suppose, the first stage in the breaking up of the old standards of taste was the invention of the 'picturesque.' A picturesque object may be defined as a thing which has some quality or qualities in excess of the normal. The nature of the excessive quality is almost a matter of indifference. Thus, even an excess of dirtiness is sufficient to render an object picturesque. The ideally picturesque object or scene possesses several excessive qualities in violent contrast one with another—for example, excess of gloom contrasting with excess of light, excess of magnificence with excess of squalor.

The quaint may be defined as the picturesque made smaller and touched with the comic. Those little old houses which Dickens so loved to describe—all holes and corners and curious accidents —are typical pieces of quaintness. There is always something snug and homely about the quaint, something even, in a comic way, slightly

virtuous—funnily good, like Tom Pinch in
Martin Chuzzlewit. It was the Victorian middle
classes who erected quaintness into a standard of
aesthetic excellence. Their love of it, coupled
with their love of the picturesque, permitted them
to admire a vast number of things which have
practically no connection with art at all. What
I may call 'arty-craftiness' or 'peasantry' is a
Tolstoyan derivation from the quaint.

The great invention of more recent years has
been the 'amusing.' In origin this is a highly
sophisticated, upper-class standard of value. All
bad art, whose badness is a positive and not a
merely negative quality of respectable dulness,
may be said to be amusing. For instance, Wordsworth, when he writes badly, is not at all amusing.
Moore, on the other hand, is ; for Moore's badness is of the period, highly coloured, mannered
and mincing. The badness of Wordsworth, like
his goodness, is of all time. The *Ecclesiastical
Sonnets* are absolute bathos, just as the finest
passages in the *Prelude* and *Excursion* are absolute
poetry.

A highly developed sense of the amusing in art
is now extremely common. Few of those who
take any conscious interest in the arts are now
without it. Amusingness has even come to have

a commercial value ; dealers find that they can get good prices for the *papier mâché* furniture of the eighteen-fifties, for the wax flowers and statuettes of the age of Louis-Philippe. The people who collect these objects appear to derive as much satisfaction from them—for a time at any rate—as they would from the most austerely graceful Heppelwhite or the choicest fourteenth-century ivories. And there is no reason, of course, why they should not, provided that they continue to recognize the fact that Heppelwhite is better than Victorian *papier mâché* and that mediaeval ivories are more beautiful than wax flowers. But the trouble is that this recognition is not always so complete or so prompt as it should be. That is the great danger attendant on the cult of the amusing ; it makes its votaries forget that there are such things as the beautiful and the sublime. In the end Erasmus Darwin comes to be preferred to Wordsworth, Longhi to Giotto. Indirectly, it is the Pierian spring that is responsible.

Part IV

BY THE WAY

'WHAT I love best in all the world,' says Browning in *De Gustibus*, 'is a castle, precipice-encurled, in a gash of the wind-grieved Apennine.' *De Gustibus*, indeed. I take the hint and shall not argue the point. Suffice it to say that, though I like the poem, I cannot share the poet's tastes. A castle in the Apennine would come quite low in the list of the things I love. A palace in Rome, a villa just outside the gates of Siena, even a motor caravan would stand higher. For the epithet which Browning applies to the Apennine is only too appropriate. He himself, no doubt, enjoyed being grieved by the wind. I can imagine him, with bent head, tunnelling his way through one of those hellish blasts which come hooting down, in spring and winter, through the gashes between the hills. He would feel exhilarated by the effort ; his struggle against the elements would elate him and he would return to his castle to write some more than ordinarily hearty paean in praise of passion and energy— passion for passion's sake, energy admirable, not so much for its direction as for its volume. Such, I am sure, were the effects of the wind on Browning ; it confirmed him in his blustering optimism.

In me, on the other hand, the wind of the Apennines begets nothing but neuralgia and the profoundest depression. It is not *Prospice* that I should write in the precipice-encurled castello ; it is something in the style of the *City of Dreadful Night*.

That I am not exaggerating the horrors of the wind among the Apennines is proved by the fact that it has been found necessary, for the convenience and even the safety of travellers, to protect the most exposed places of the principal passes with high walls. I remember in particular one section of the main road from Florence to Bologna which is flanked for hundreds of yards by an immense parapet, like the great wall of China. The road at this point, which is between two and three thousand feet above the sea, cuts across the head of a deep and narrow valley, through which there sucks a perpetual draught. Even in summer, on halcyon days, you can hear as you pass under the lee of the wall, a melancholy wailing of the winds overhead. But on rough days in winter, in the spring and autumn, the air is full of fearful noises, as though the gates of hell had been opened and the lost souls were making holiday. What happened to travellers who passed that way before, some hundred years ago, a beneficent Grand-Ducal government built the wall, I shudder to think. They must often have been, quite literally, blown off the road.

We passed that way once in March. The Italian spring, which is not so different from the spring in other countries, was inclement that year and icy. In Florence the sun shone fitfully between huge clouds. Snow still lay in patches on Monte Morello. The breeze was nipping. ' Are the passes free of snow ? ' we asked at the garage where we stopped to fill our petrol tank. Animated by that typically Italian desire to give an answer that will please the questioner, the garage man assured us that the road was perfectly clear. And he said it with such conviction that we imagined, as northerners would naturally imagine, that he knew. Nothing is more charming than southern courtesy, southern sympathy and the southern desire to please. The heart is touched by the kindly interest which the Italians take in your affairs ; you love them for their courteous inquisitiveness ; they make you at home immediately, treat you at once as a human being and do their best to please you. It is delightful. But sometimes they are really too sympathetic by half. For in order not to contradict you or give you a moment's pain by disputing the accuracy of your ideas, they will tell you what you want to hear rather than what it would be of real use to you to hear. At the same time their own self-esteem will not permit them to confess a blank ignorance ; so that they will rather tell you something incorrect than tell you nothing at all. Thus, when the garage man told us that there was no snow on the road from Florence to Bologna, he said so first, because he saw that we wanted to go to Bologna and that we should have been disappointed if it had been impossible and, second, because it was pleasanter for him to say ' No snow ' with conviction than confess (which was the truth) that he hadn't the faintest notion whether there was snow or not.

We believed him and set out. The road rises steeply from Florence, climbs to twelve or fifteen hundred feet and then plunges down again into that long flat-bottomed valley locked in the midst of the hills, the Mugello. By the time we had reached it the sun had entirely disappeared, and the sky above us was one vast yellowish-white snowcloud. Looking at the various castelli one passes by the way, I found Browning's predilections more than ever incomprehensible.

Between Florence and Bologna there are two passes : the Futa and, five or six miles further on, the pass of Raticosa. It is near the top of the Futa that the Grand Dukes built the bulwark against the wind. It was strengthened, that day, by heaps of driven snow. Below and above, the slopes were deep in snow. In the midst of all this whiteness the road wound onwards and upwards like a muddy snake.

Under the lee of the wall we halted and took photographs of the Italian scenery. The air was calm where we stood and seemed in its stillness almost warm. But just above us, on a level with the top of the wall, was the wind. The snow-flakes that it carried made its speed visible. It filled the ears with sound. I was reminded, as I stood there, of a rather ludicrous and deplorable version of *David Copperfield*, which Beerbohm Tree used sometimes to stage at His Majesty's. Tree himself acted two parts—Micawber and Peggotty ; the former, I may add parenthetically, very well indeed (for he was an admirable come-dian), the latter, in his more pathetic manner, with less success. But let that pass. Dressed as Peggotty, Tree never made an entrance without the wind ; it was in the bluff nautical part. Every time he opened the door of his ship cottage on the sands of Yarmouth there came from the outer darkness a noise like the witches' sabbath.

It never blew less than a full gale during the whole run of *David Copperfield*. Whoo-oo-oo-oo-oo —crescendo and decrescendo. In the dress-circle ladies reached for their furs, men turned up the collars of their coats. It was horrible. I had hoped then that I should never hear a wind like that outside His Majesty's. And I never did till that icy March day when we paused beneath the Grand-Ducal wall on the road from Florence to Bologna. There, for the first time, I heard nature rivalling Sir Herbert's art. A perfect site, I reflected, for the Castello Browning.

At Pietramala, which lies just under the pass of the Raticosa, we stopped at the little inn for lunch. The idlers who gathered immediately and as though by magic round our machine—for even at Pietramala, even in the snow, there were leisured car-fanciers to whom the arrival of a ten-horse-power Citroën was an event—lost no time in telling us that the road on the further side of the pass was blocked with wind-driven snow. We went in to our lunch feeling a little depressed —a little annoyed, too, with the garage man at Florence. The inn-keeper, however, was re-assuring ; gangs of men, he told us, were to be sent out as soon as the dinner hour was over from Pietramala and the village on the other side of the pass. By four o'clock the road would be clear ; we should be in Bologna before dark. When we asked if the road by Firenzuola and Imola were open, he shook his head. For the second time that day we believed.

The inn-keeper's motives for not telling the truth were different from those that actuated the man at the garage. For the latter had lied out of misplaced politeness and pride ; the inn-keeper on the contrary, lied merely out of self-interest. He wanted to make us stay the night. He was perfectly successful. At four o'clock we set out. At the top of the pass the snow lay a yard deep across the road, and there was not a shoveller to be seen. We returned. The inn-keeper was astonished : what, no shovellers ? He could hardly believe it. But to-morrow morning the road would infallibly be cleared. We decided to stay the night.

I had taken with me on that journey the second volume of the *Encyclopaedia Britannica*—And.-Aus. It is a capital volume from which one can derive much useful knowledge about Angiosperms, the Anglican Communion, Angling, Anthrax, Aphasia, Apples, Arrowroot, Asia, Aurora Borealis and Australia, not to mention Anthropology, Archeology, Architecture, Art,

SALEM COLLEGE LIBRARY
Winston-Salem, North Carolina

Astrology and Astronomy. I started hopefully on Animal Worship. 'The bear,' I learned, 'enjoys a large measure of respect from all savage races that come in contact with it.' From me, that evening, he got a large measure of envy. I thought of Mr. Belloc's rhyme:

> The Polar Bear is unaware
> Of cold that cuts me through:
> For why? He has a coat of hair.
> I wish I had one too!

For in spite of the fire, in spite of great-coats, it was appallingly cold. 'The products of the cow,' I read on, and was charmed by the compendious euphemism, 'are important in magic.' But I got no further; it was too cold even to read. To this day I remain ignorant of the feelings of the Thlinkit Indians towards the crow, of the Kalangs towards the dog and the Siamese towards white elephants. And if I do happen to know that the Hottentot god, Cagn, is incarnated in the praying mantis, Ngo, that is due to the fact that I took the same volume with me on another tour during the summer, when the evenings were less inclement and the mind was free to devote itself to higher things than the problem of mere self-preservation.

It was cold enough in the sitting-room; but

the horror only really began when we went to
bed.   For the bedrooms of the inn were without
fireplaces ;   there was no possibility of heating
them.   In those bedrooms one could have preserved mutton indefinitely.   Still dressed in all
the woolly garments we possessed, we got into our
stony beds.   Outside the wind continued to howl
among the hills.   While the sheets were yet un-
thawed, sleep was out of the question.   I lay
awake listening to the noise of the wind and
wondering what would be the effect of the hurri-
cane on those flaming jets of natural gas for which
Pietramala is renowned.   Would the wind blow
out those giant will-o'-the-wisps ?   Or would
they burn on in spite of it ?   The thought of
flames was comforting ;   I dwelt on them with
a certain complaisance.

They are not uncommon, these jets of fire,
among the northern Apennines.   Salsomaggiore,
for example, owes its coat of arms, a salamander
among the flames, to its fountains of natural gas.
It is in this gaseous form alone that the hydro-
carbons of the Apennines make their appearance
at the centre of the chain.   On the outer slopes
they are to be found in the more commercially
useful form of petroleum, which is now extracted
in small quantities from the foothills in the neigh-

bourhood of Piacenza, Reggio and Modena. Who knows, we may yet live to see the towers of Canossa rivalled by the wooden castles of the derricks on the slopes below.

The shutters rattled, the wind howled. Decidedly, no fire could burn in the teeth of such a blast. Poor *ignes fatui* ! how welcome we should have made them in this ice-house ! How tenderly, like vestals, we should have cherished any flame, however fatuous !

From thinking of those flames and wishing that I had them in the room with me, I went on to wonder why it was that the gas-fires of Pietramala should be so oddly familiar to me. Had I read about them ? Had I recently heard them mentioned in conversation, or what ? I racked my brains. And then suddenly I remembered; it was in Bence Jones's *Life and Letters of Faraday* that I had read of Pietramala.

One very wet day in the autumn of 1814 two rather queer English tourists alighted from their chaise in this squalid little village of Pietramala. One was approaching middle age, the other still a very young man. Their names were Sir Humphry Davy and Michael Faraday. They had been out of England almost exactly a year. For it was in the year 1813, just before the news of the battle of Leipzig had reached Paris, that they crossed into France. To us it seems in the natural order of things that science and religion should be national affairs, that clergymen should scream 'Hurrah and Hallelujah' and chemists cheer for the flag and H_2SO_4. But it was not always so. God and the works of God were once considered international. God was the first to be nationalized; after the Reformation he once more became frankly tribal. But science and even art were still above patriotism. During the eighteenth century France and England exchanged ideas almost as freely as cannon balls. French scientific expeditions were allowed to pass in safety between the English fleets; Sterne was welcomed enthusiastically by his country's enemies. The tradition lingered on even into the eighteen hundreds. Napoleon gave medals to English men of science; and when, in 1813, Sir Humphry Davy asked for leave to travel on the Continent, his request was granted at once. He was received in Paris with the highest honours, was made a member of the Institute, and in spite of the intolerable rudeness and arrogance which he habitually displayed, he was treated throughout his stay in France with the most perfect courtesy. In our more enlightened twentieth century he would have been shot as a spy or interned.

Restless and erratic, Davy hurried across Europe in search of scientific truth. All was fish that came to his net. At Genoa he made electric experiments on the torpedo fish. At Florence he borrowed the great burning-glass of the Grand Dukes and, with its aid, set a diamond on fire. At Rome he analysed the pigments employed by the artists of antiquity. At Naples he made experiments on iodine and excursions up Vesuvius. With him went Michael Faraday as 'assistant in experiments and writing.' Lady Davy, however, tried to use him as courier and confidential servant as well. Young Faraday found the position a little trying. It was only the consciousness that he was being given an unrivalled opportunity to educate himself that decided him to keep his post. Sir Humphry's character might not be entirely estimable (indeed, Faraday was known to remark in later years that ' the greatest of all his great advantages was that he had had, in Davy, a model to teach him what he should avoid ') ; but he was, undoubtedly, a mine of scientific learning. To be with him constantly, as Faraday was, during those eighteen months of travel, was a liberal education. Young Faraday knew it and put up with Lady D.

At Pietramala, then, they stopped in the pouring rain—and doubtless in the howling wind as well—to look at the natural fireworks. Specimens of the gas were bottled and taken down to Florence for analysis. Sir Humphry concluded, correctly, that it was a light hydrocarburet, pure.

To this desolate little village on the crest of the Apennines Faraday devotes a couple of pages in his journal. To Florence, except in so far as it was a town where there were facilities for making experiments, he gives no space at all. Faraday paid little attention to the works of man, however beautiful. It was the works of God that interested him. There is a magnificent consistency about him. All that he writes in his journal or letters is perfectly in character. He is always the natural philosopher. To discover truth is his sole aim and interest. His purpose is unalterably fixed. He never allows himself to be distracted —not by art, which he almost completely ignores ; not by politics, which in the tremendous closing scenes of the Napoleonic drama he mentions casually once or twice, not at all by the delights of casual social intercourse, though he always found time for friendship—but pursues his course steadily, perseverantly, modestly, disinterestedly, and withal triumphantly as a conquering man of genius.

Outside science his great interest was religion. The battle between science and dogmatic theology, which was waged during the latter half of the nineteenth century, created an impression, which still survives, that there is a certain radical incompatibility between science and religion. History shows that, as a matter of fact, no such incompatibility exists. If we read the biographies of the three most genial (in the French sense) men of science that England has produced—Sir Isaac Newton, Faraday and James Clerk Maxwell—we shall find that all three were profoundly religious. Sir Isaac devoted the greater part of a long life to the interpretation of Biblical prophecy. Faraday was an earnest and ardent Christian of the Sandemanian sect. Clerk Maxwell was a great mystic as well as a great man of science ; there are letters of his which show him to have been of the company of Boehme and Swedenborg (himself, by the way, a scientific man of great distinction). There is nothing in all this that should surprise us. ' An infidel astronomer is mad ' ; tempered, this piece of rhetoric is something like a truth. For it is certainly impossible to study nature at all closely without becoming convinced of the extraordinary strangeness and mysteriousness of the familiar world in which the mass of human beings unquestioningly pass their lives. The further our knowledge extends and the more completely we realize its implications, the more mysterious this universe is seen to be. A man must be crass and unimaginative indeed if he can study the intricacies of life, the movements of the stars, the intimate constitution of matter without feeling from time to time a sense of awe and amazement. In the ranks of the professional scientists such men undoubtedly find their place; there are unimaginative men in all professions, from that of the jockey to that of the bishop. But they are not, in general, the best at their jobs. Without imagination, without sensitiveness it is impossible to be a successful man of science. It would be difficult to find any great scientific man who had not been touched by this sense of wonder at the strangeness of things. It betrays itself in different ways according to the upbringing and temperament of those who feel it. In some, as quiet and orthodox religion; in others, unwilling to commit themselves definitely about the nature of the mystery which surrounds them, as agnosticism; in others again (Clerk Maxwell and

Swedenborg are examples) the man of science is endowed with the peculiar mental qualities of the mystic ; in yet other cases we find men possessing these same mystical qualities, but unrefined and somehow coarse (for there are good mystics and poor mystics just as there are good and poor artists), and then we have, not Clerk Maxwell with his delicate and beautiful mysticism, but Newton the interpreter of the prophetic books. For Faraday the corollary and complement of science was protestant Christianity. His sense of wonder, his awe in face of the beautiful mystery of the world, expressed itself in the terms of Sandemanian meetings and Bible reading. He stands in the scale of mystics somewhere about half-way between Maxwell and Newton, not very highly gifted but at the same time not vulgarly gifted, a sort of Andrea del Sarto between Giotto on the one hand and Caravaggio on the other. A Cherubini between Mozart and Strauss.

That king who, in Anatole France's fable, was only to be cured of his melancholy by putting on the shirt of a happy man, would have been well advised to apply to Faraday. A shirt of his would have been specific against the king's malady. For if any man was happy it was surely he. All his life long he did, professionally, the things he

desired to do. To know, to discover the truth—
that was his desire. And it is a desire whose fulfilment does not lead to disappointment and
boredom, as does the fulfilment of almost every
other human longing. For there is no end to
truth ; each part of it reveals, when found, yet
other parts to be discovered. The man who
desires knowledge knows no satiety, for the knowable is perpetually new. He might live innumerable lives and never grow weary. True, the
knowable world is not everything. There is
also the world of feelings ; there is also that
which is humanly unknowable. In our relation
to these two worlds there is plenty of scope for
unhappiness. But Faraday was also emotionally
happy. His marriage was an unqualified success;
he had good friends ; the tenour of his life was
even and he did not desire more than what he
possessed. He was equally fortunate in his relation to the unknowable. The problems of life,
as they are called, never troubled him. The
religion in which he was brought up offered a
solution of them in advance ; he passed through
no crisis such as that which drove Tolstoy almost
to suicide. It is interesting to note that he separated the domain of science sharply from that of
religion, the knowable from the unknowable.

'Not *how* the world is, is the mystical, but *that* it is,' says Wittgenstein. And again : 'For an answer which cannot be expressed the question too cannot be expressed. The riddle does not exist. . . . The solution of the problem of life is seen in the vanishing of this problem. (Is not this the reason why men to whom after long doubting the sense of life became clear, could not then say wherein this sense consisted ?)' Faraday was happy in that he never doubted, never tried to put an inexpressible question for which there is no possible answer. How the world is, he set himself to discover, with more success than attends most investigators. He did not torture his intellect with the question why or what it is. His religion offered him the explanation why ; or to be more exact (for there is no explanation) it helped him to ' contemplate the world *sub specie aeterni*, as a limited whole.' ' The feeling of the world as a limited whole is the mystical feeling.' Faraday had that feeling ; not perhaps in its most exquisite form, but had it genuinely. His relations with the unknowable therefore were as satisfactory as his relations with what can be known.

Among the natural philosophers Faraday is by no means unique in his happiness. Indeed, as a class, I should say that men of science were happier than other men. *A priori*, and almost by definition, they ought to be. And when one reads their lives one finds that in point of fact they generally were happy. How satisfactory these lives of born men of science always are ! There is an integrity about these men, a unity of purpose that to the rest of us poor distracted mortals seems wonderfully enviable and wonderfully beautiful.

If I could be born again and choose what I should be in my next existence, I should desire to be a man of science—not accidentally but by nature, inevitably a man of science. Fate might offer other alternatives—to have power or wealth, be a king or a statesman. These glittering temptations I should have small difficulty in rejecting ; for my objection to the irritating turmoil of practical life is even stronger than my love of money or power, and since these cannot be obtained without plunging into practical life, I can sacrifice them cheerfully. It is easy to make a virtue of psychological necessity. The only thing that might make me hesitate would be an offer by fate of artistic genius. But even if I could be Shakespeare, I think I should still choose to be Faraday. True, the posthumous glory of Shakespeare is greater than that of Faraday ; men still read *Macbeth* but not (even if they happen to be electricians) — the *Experimental Researches in Electricity*. The work of a man of science is a creation on which others build ; it has implications, it grows. If we want to know about electricity, we read what the contemporary successors and disciples of Faraday have to say about it. But *Macbeth* is a thing in itself, not a discovery on which other men can improve. There is no such thing as progress in art. Every artist begins at the beginning. The man of science, on the other hand, begins where his predecessor left off. Opinions and ideas change, under the weight of accumulated experience, from age to age. The instinctive, emotional side of man, being hereditary, remains the same. The man of science provides the experience that changes the ideas of the race ; in course of time his discoveries are superseded. The artist does not go out of date because he works with materials that do not change. Lyrics composed by a palaeolithic poet would still be moving. But the views of a palaeolithic astronomer would possess, for us, a merely historical and academic interest.

And yet in spite of all this I would still rather be Faraday than Shakespeare. Posthumous fame brings nobody much satisfaction this side of the grave ; and though the consciousness that one possesses a great artistic talent must be profoundly satisfying, though the free employment of it must be a source of happiness, it seems to me that the possession and employment of a scientific talent must be still more satisfying. For the artist, whose function is the apt expression and the conveyance to others of the common human emotions, must fatally pass much of his life in the emotional world of human contacts. His reflections upon the world, his personal reactions to contacts—these form the subject matter of his art. The world in which the man of science passes the professional part of his life is non-human, has nothing to do with personal relationships and emotional reactions. We are all subdued to what we work in ; and I personally would rather be subdued to intellectual contemplation than to emotion, would rather use my soul professionally for knowing than for feeling.

One of the minor disadvantages of being a great artist is the fact that the artist enjoys a considerable social prestige. Art is the subject of snobbery to a far greater extent than science. The presence of a well-known poet or painter is felt to give distinction to a dinner-party. Hostesses rarely ask one to meet bio-chemists, however distinguished. The reason for this is simple ;

all men and women imagine that they can appreciate the arts—and up to a point, of course, actually
can—while the number who can understand the
technicalities of science is remarkably small.
(Vainly, alas, I wish that I myself belonged to
that minority.) To this is due the enviable
immunity of the men of science from the intrusion
of frivolous bores. The artist, on the other hand,
is one of the favourite quarries of the unemployed
rich ; a good specimen is worth at least an am-
bassador, almost an Indian prince. If the artist
is a man of strong character he will find the atten-
tions of the lion-hunters not dangerous, indeed,
but profoundly exasperating. They are only
dangerous to those who allow themselves to be
caught. It is pleasant to be flattered ; and if one
likes to waste time, there is no easier way of doing
so than in casual social intercourse. The artist
who succumbs to social temptations loses everything : his time, his integrity, his sense of proportion, the very hope of achieving anything
important. He is the more unfortunate in being
exposed to them.

Towards morning when, like a mutton chop
on a cold plate, I had a little thawed my bed, the
phantoms of Michael Faraday and Sir Humphry
Davy departed, leaving me alone with my re-

pressed wishes. What they may have been, I don't know. But at any rate they fulfilled themselves, ideally and symbolically, in a confused nightmare of motor cars and snowdrifts.

The wind was still blowing when I woke up. We spent the forenoon shivering in the sitting-room of the inn. Every few minutes the land-lord came in with fresh news about the state of affairs on the pass. Telephone messages had arrived from Florence and Bologna ; an army of shovellers was being mobilized ; now it was on the move ; a man who had just come down from the pass had seen them at work ; by two o'clock the road could not fail to be clear. After giving us each item of news, he bowed, smiled, rubbed his hands and went back to his kitchen to invent the next. He had a fertile imagination.

Fitfully, I read about the Armenian Church. But my interest was languid. I was too cold even to feel a proper enthusiasm over the dis-covery that 'the old sacrificial hymns were probably obscene and certainly nonsensical.' Re-membering that phrase in subsequent summers, I have been delighted by it. How well, how pithily it describes not merely the old sacrificial hymns of pre-Christian Armenia, but a whole mass of modern art and self-styled science—the greater part of psycho-analytic literature, for example, the music of Schreker, most expressionist painting, *Ulysses*, and so on. As for the less 'modern' pseudo-sciences and pseudo-art, from spiritualism to commercial fiction—these do not even possess the saving grace of obscenity; they are merely nonsensical.

The morning passed; it was time for lunch. After a meal of spaghetti and broiled goat, we felt a little stronger and a little less cold. 'How are things on the pass?' we asked. But our host seemed suddenly to have lost his omniscience and with it his optimism. He did not know what was happening and he advised us to wait for a little. By five o'clock, however, all would undoubtedly be well. And the road by Firenzuola? That was hopeless; he was certain of that. He left us wondering what to do; whether to wait, whether to return to Florence—what? We were still in a state of painful uncertainty when a heaven-sent messenger in the form of a man with a horse and trap stopped at the inn door. We appealed to him. A miracle! Not only did he know the truth; he also imparted his knowledge in a plain unvarnished way. No shovellers, he assured us, were working on the pass; nor would any be sent there till the wind had changed (for when the wind was blowing in this particular direction, the snow was carried back on to the road as soon as it had been taken off). The wind might change this evening, of course ; but on the other hand it might only change next week. But if we wanted to go to Bologna, why hadn't we taken the Firenzuola road ? Yes, why not ? said the landlord, who had joined us and was listening to the conversation. Why not take the Firenzuola road ? He had seen that the game was up and that there was now no further hope of getting us to stay another night. Why not ? We looked at him significantly, in silence. He smiled back, imperviously good-humoured, and retired to compile his bill.

We set out. The sky was white and full of cloudy movement. Here and there the white mountains were scarred with black, where the precipices were too steep to allow the snow to lie. From La Casetta we slid down the break-neck road that twists down into the valley of the Santerno. Within its walls Firenzuola was black, ancient and grim. From Firenzuola the road follows the Santerno. The river has tunnelled a winding passage through the mountains. The valley is deep and narrow ; here and there road and river run between perpendicular walls of

rock, banded slantwise with the lines of tilted
stratification. Slowly the valley broadens out,
the mountains degenerate into bare bleak downs.
At the foot of the hills is the plain, narrowed here
between the mountains and the sea, but expanding
and expanding as one travels northwards into the
immense unbroken flatness of the Po valley.

At Imola we turned into the great Via Emilia
that runs in an undeviating straight line from
Rimini to Piacenza. What cities are strung
along that white stretched thread ! Cesena, Forlì,
Faenza, Imola, Bologna, Reggio, Modena, Parma
—bead after precious bead.

It was dark when we entered Bologna and the
streets were full of maskers. It was the last
day of carnival.

We nosed our way through the crowd, hooting.
' Maschere ! ' the maskers shouted as we passed ;
and in our goggles and mufflers, we too seemed
dressed for carnival. It was a feeble show ; a
few young women in dominoes, a few noisy
students in fancy dress—that was all. I thought
of the brilliant shows and masquerades of the past.
Charming, no doubt ; but one should not regret
them. For shows and masquerades are symptoms
of bad government. Tyrants pass all their lives
at the centre of a gorgeous ballet. An oppressed

populace, too poor to pay for amusements of its own, is kept in good humour by these royal theatricals, which are free of charge. And in the course of periodical Saturnalia slaves are able to sublimate their revolutionary feelings in sportive licence. If carnival has decayed, so too has oppression. And where people have pence enough to go to the cinema, there is no need for kings and popes to stage their ballets. Still, it was a very poor show; I felt they might have celebrated our arrival in Bologna a little more worthily.

Rᴇꜰᴏʀᴍᴇʀs look forward to a time when efficient social organization and perfected machinery
will do away with the necessity for severe and
prolonged labour, making possible for all men and
women an amount of leisure such as is enjoyed
at the present day only by a privileged few.
Nobody, in that golden age, will need to work
more than four or five hours a day. The rest
of every man's time will be his own, to do with
whatsoever he likes.

It is difficult for any sensitive person not to
sympathize with these aspirations. One must be
most arrogantly certain of one's own super-
manhood before one can complacently accept the
slavery on which the possibility of being a super-
man is based. Poor Nietzsche ended by signing
his letters ' Nietzsche Caesar ' and died in a
madhouse. Perhaps that is the price that must
be paid—at any rate by the intelligent ; for the
placidly stupid never pay, just as they never
receive, anything—for an unfaltering conviction
of superiority.

But sympathy with an ideal need not make
the sympathizer uncritical of it ; one may feel
strongly, but one must not therefore cease to think.

The majority of human beings are oppressed by excessive labour of the most senseless kind. That fact may, and indeed should, arouse our indignation and our pity. But these emotions must not prevent us from criticizing the project of those who wish to change the present state of things. The social reformers desire to see a dispensation under which all men will have as much, or nearly as much leisure as is enjoyed by the leisured classes to-day. We may be permitted to doubt, for all our sympathy, whether the consummation is really, after all, so much to be desired.

Let us begin by asking one simple question : What is it proposed that human beings shall do with the leisure which social reorganization and perfected machinery are to give them ?

Prophets of the future give fundamentally the same answer to this question, with slight variations according to their different tastes. Henri Poincaré, for example, imagined that the human beings of the future would fill their long leisures by 'contemplating the laws of nature.' Mr. Bernard Shaw is of much the same opinion. Having ceased, by the time they are four years old, to take any interest in such childish things as love, art and the society of their fellow beings, the Ancients in *Back to Methuselah* devote their indefinitely prolonged existences to meditating on the mysterious and miraculous beauty of the cosmos. Mr. H. G. Wells portrays in *Men like Gods* a race of athletic chemists and mathematical physicists who go about naked and, unlike Mr. Shaw's austerer Ancients, make free love in a rational manner between the experiments. They also take an interest in the arts and are not above playing games.

These three answers to our question are typical. Different prophets may differ in their estimate of the relative importance of the various activities which make up what is generally known as 'the higher life'; but all agree that the lives of our leisured posterity will be high. They will eagerly make themselves acquainted with 'the best that has been thought or said' about everything; they will listen to concerts of the classiest music; they will practise the arts and handicrafts (at any rate until the time comes when even these occupations seem childish); they will study the sciences, philosophy, mathematics, and meditate on the lovely mystery of the world in which they live.

In a word, these leisured masses of a future which there is no reason to believe enormously remote—indeed, our grandchildren may live to see the establishment of the four-hour day—will

234

do all the things which our leisured classes of the present time so conspicuously fail to do.

How many rich and leisured people are there now living, who spend their time contemplating the laws of nature ? I cannot say ; all I know is that I rarely meet them. Many of the leisured, it is true, devote themselves to the patronage and even the amateur practice of the arts. But any one who has moved among rich ' artistic ' people knows how much of this cultivation of the arts is due to snobbery, how shallow and insincere their loudly voiced enthusiasms mostly are. The leisured classes take up art for the same reasons as they take up bridge—to escape from boredom. With sport and love-making, art helps to fill up the vacuum of their existence.

At Monte Carlo and Nice one meets the rich whose dominant interests are play and love. Two millions, according to my guide-book, annually visit Monte Carlo alone. Seven-eighths of the whole leisured population of Europe must con- centrate themselves yearly on that strip of the coast. Five thousand jazz bands play daily for their delectation. A hundred thousand motor vehicles transport them from one place to another at great speed. Huge joint-stock companies offer them every kind of distraction, from roulette to

235

golf. Legions of prostitutes assemble from all parts of the globe and enthusiastic amateurs of the gentle passion abound. For four months in the year the French Riviera is an earthly paradise. When the four months are over, the leisured rich return to their northerly homes, where they find awaiting them less splendid, but quite authentic *succursales* of the paradise they have left behind.

The leisured rich at Monte Carlo are those, I have said, whose chief resources against ennui or serious thoughts are love and play. Many of them are also 'artistic.' But it is not, I think, at Monte Carlo that the best specimens of the artistic rich are to be found. To see them at their best one must go to Florence. Florence is the home of those who cultivate with an equal ardour Mah-jongg and a passion for Fra Angelico. Over tea and crumpets they talk, if they are too old for love themselves, of their lascivious juniors; but they also make sketches in water colour and read the *Little Flowers of St. Francis.*

I must not, in justice to the leisured rich, omit to mention that respectable minority of them who occupy themselves with works of charity (not to mention tyranny), with politics, with local administration and occasionally with scholarly or scientific studies. I hesitate to use the word 'service';

for it has been held up so frequently as an ideal and by such a riff-raff of newspaper proprietors, hard-headed business men and professional moralists from the Y.M.C.A., that it has lost all real significance. The 'ideal of service' is achieved, according to our modern messiahs, by those who do efficient and profitable business with just enough honesty to keep them out of gaol. Plain shopkeeping is thus exalted into a beautiful virtue. The ideal of service which animates the best part of the English leisured class has nothing to do with the ideals of service so frequently mentioned by advertisers in American magazines. If I had not made this clear, my praise might have been thought, if not positively insulting, at least most damnably faint.

There exists, then, an admirable minority. But even when the minority and its occupations are duly taken into account, it cannot honestly be said that the leisured classes of the present time, or indeed of any historical period of which we have knowledge, provide a very good advertisement for leisure. The contemplation of richly leisured life in Monte Carlo and even in artistic Florence is by no means cheering or elevating.

Nor are we much reassured when we consider the occupations of the unleisured poor during those brief hours of repose allowed them between their work and their sleep. Watching other people play games, looking at cinema films, reading newspapers and indifferent fiction, listening to radio concerts and gramophone records and going from place to place in trains and omnibuses—these, I suppose, are the principal occupations of the working-man's leisure. Their cheapness is all that distinguishes them from the diversions of the rich. Prolong the leisure and what will happen? There will have to be more cinemas, more newspapers, more bad fiction, more radios and more cheap automobiles. If wealth and education increase with the leisure, then there will have to be more Russian Ballets as well as more movies, more *Timeses* as well as more *Daily Mails*, more casinos as well as more bookies and football matches, more expensive operas as well as more gramophone records, more Hugh Walpoles as well as more Nat Goulds. Acting on the same organisms the same causes may be expected to produce the same effects. And for all ordinary purposes, and so far as historical time is concerned, human nature is practically unchanging; the organism does remain the same. *Argal*, as Launcelot Gobbo would have said. . . .

This being so, we must further assume that

increase of leisure will be accompanied by a cor-
respondingly increased incidence of those spiritual
maladies—ennui, restlessness, spleen and general
world-weariness—which afflict and have always
afflicted the leisured classes now and in the past.

Another result of increased leisure, provided
that it is accompanied by a tolerably high standard
of living, will be a very much increased interest on
the part of what is now the working class in all
matters of an amorous nature. Love, in all its
complicated luxuriance, can only flourish in a
society composed of well-fed, unemployed people.
Examine the literature which has been written by
and for members of the leisured classes and compare it with popular working-class literature.
Compare *La Princesse de Clèves* with *The Pilgrim's
Progress*, Proust with Charles Garvice, Chaucer's
Troilus and Cressida with the ballads. It becomes at once sufficiently evident that the leisured
classes do take and have always taken a much
keener and, I might say, more professional interest in love than the workers. A man cannot
work hard and at the same time conduct elaborate
love affairs. Making love, at any rate in the
style in which unemployed women desire it to be
made, is a whole-time job. It demands both
energy and leisure. Now energy and leisure are

precisely the things which a hard worker lacks. Reduce his working hours and he will have both.

If, to-morrow or a couple of generations hence, it were made possible for all human beings to lead the life of leisure which is now led only by a few, the results, so far as I can see, would be as follows: There would be an enormous increase in the demand for such time-killers and substitutes for thought as newspapers, films, fiction, cheap means of communication and wireless telephones ; to put it in more general terms, there would be an increase in the demand for sport and art. The interest in the fine art of love-making would be widely extended. And enormous numbers of people, hitherto immune from these mental and moral diseases, would be afflicted by ennui, depression and universal dissatisfaction.

The fact is that, brought up as they are at present, the majority of human beings can hardly fail to devote their leisure to occupations which, if not positively vicious, are at least stupid, futile and, what is worse, secretly realized to be futile.

To Tolstoy the whole idea of universal leisure seemed absurd and even wicked. The social reformers who held up the attainment of universal leisure as an ideal he regarded as madmen. They aspired to make all men like those rich, idle, urban people among whom he had passed his youth and whom he so profoundly despised. He regarded them as conspirators against the welfare of the race.

What seemed to Tolstoy important was not that the workers should get more leisure but that the leisured should work. For him the social ideal was labour for all in natural surroundings. He wanted to see all men and women living on the land and subsisting on the produce of the fields that they themselves had tilled. The makers of Utopias are fond of prophesying that a time will come when men will altogether abandon agriculture and live on synthetic foods ; to Tolstoy the idea was utterly revolting. But though he was doubtless right to be revolted, the prophets of synthetic food are probably better seers than he. Mankind is more likely to become urbanized than completely ruralized. But these probabilities do not concern us here. What concerns us is Tolstoy's opinion of leisure.

Tolstoy's dislike of leisure was due to his own experience as an idle youth and his observation of other rich and leisured men and women. He concluded that, as things are, leisure is generally more of a curse than a blessing. It is difficult, when one visits Monte Carlo or the other earthly paradises of the leisured, not to agree with him. Most minds will only do work under compulsion. Leisure is only profitable to those who desire, even without compulsion, to do mental work. In a society entirely composed of such active minds leisure would be an unmixed blessing. Such a society has never existed and does not at the present exist. Can it ever be called into being ?

Those who believe that all the defects of nature may be remedied by suitable nurture will reply in the affirmative. And indeed it is sufficiently obvious that the science of education is still in a very rudimentary condition. We possess a sufficient knowledge of physiology to be able to devise gymnastic exercises that shall develop the body to its highest attainable efficiency. But our knowledge of the mind, and particularly of the growing mind, is far less complete ; and even such knowledge as we possess is not systematically or universally applied to the problems of education. Our minds are like the flabby bodies of sedentary city dwellers—inefficient and imperfectly developed. With a vast number of people intellectual development ceases almost in childhood ; they go through life with the intellectual capacities of boys or girls of fifteen. A proper course of mental gymnastics, based on real psychological knowledge, would at least permit all minds to reach their maximum development. Splendid prospect! But our enthusiasm for education is a little cooled when we consider what *is* the maximum development attainable by the greatest number of human beings. Men born with talents are to men born without them as human beings to dogs in respect to these particular faculties. Mathematically, I am a dog compared with Newton; a dog, musically, compared with Beethoven, and a dog, artistically, compared with Giotto. Not to mention the fact that I am a dog compared to Blondin, as a tight-rope walker; a billiard-playing dog compared with Newman; a boxing dog compared with Dempsey; a wine-tasting dog compared with Ruskin's father. And so on. Even if I were perfectly educated in mathematics, music, painting, tight-rope walking, billiard playing, boxing and wine-tasting, I should only become a trained dog instead of a dog in the state of nature. The prospect fills me with only moderate satisfaction.

Education can assure to every man the maximum of mental development. But is that maximum high enough in the majority of cases to allow a whole society to live in leisure without developing

those deplorable qualities which have always characterized the leisured classes ?   I know plenty of
people who have received the best education available in the present age and employ their leisure as
though they had never been educated at all.   But
then our best education is admittedly bad (though
good enough for all the men of talent and genius
whom we possess) ; perhaps when it has been
made really efficient, these people will spend their
leisure contemplating the laws of nature.   Perhaps.   I venture to doubt it.

Mr. Wells, who is a believer in nurture, puts
his Utopia three thousand years into the future ;
Mr. Shaw, less optimistically trusting to nature
and a process of conscious evolution, removes his
to the year 30,000 A.D.   Geologically speaking,
these times are to all intent equal in their brevity.
Unfortunately, however, we are not fossils, but
men.   Even three thousand years seem, in our
eyes, an uncommonly long time.   The thought
that, three thousand or thirty thousand years
hence, human beings may, conceivably, be leading
a lovely and rational existence is only mildly comforting and feebly sustaining.   Men have a habit
of thinking only of themselves, their children and
their children's children.   And they are quite
right.   Thirty thousand years hence, all may be

well. But meanwhile that bad geological quarter of an hour which separates the present from that rosy future has got to be lived through. And I foresee that one of the minor, or even the major problems of that quarter of an hour will be the problem of leisure. By the year two thousand the six-hour day will be everywhere the rule, and the next hundred years will probably see the maximum reduced to five or even less. Nature, by then, will have had no time to change the mental habits of the race ; and nurture, though improved, will only turn dogs into trained dogs. How will men and women fill their ever-expanding leisure ? By contemplating the laws of nature, like Henri Poincaré ? Or by reading the *News of the World* ? I wonder.

THERE is a certain jovial, bouncing, hoppety little tune with which any one who has spent even a few weeks in Germany, or has been tended in childhood by a German nurse, must be very familiar. Its name is 'Ach, du lieber Augustin.' It is a merry little affair in three-four time ; in rhythm and melody so simple, that the village idiot could sing it after a first hearing ; in sentiment so innocent that the heart of the most susceptible maiden would not quicken by a beat a minute at the sound of it. Rum ti-tiddle, Um tum tum, Um tum tum, Um tum tum : Rum ti-tiddle, Um tum tum, Um tum tum, TUM. By the very frankness of its cheerful imbecility the thing disarms all criticism.

Now for a piece of history. 'Ach, du lieber Augustin' was composed in 1770, and it was the first waltz. The first waltz ! I must ask the reader to hum the tune to himself, then to think of any modern waltz with which he may be familiar. He will find in the difference between the tunes a subject richly suggestive of interesting meditations.

The difference between 'Ach, du lieber Augustin' and any waltz tune composed at any

date from the middle of the nineteenth century
onwards, is the difference between one piece
of music almost completely empty of emotional
content and another, densely saturated with
amorous sentiment, languor and voluptuousness.
The susceptible maiden who, when she hears
'Ach, du lieber Augustin,' feels no emotions
beyond a general sense of high spirits and cheer-
fulness, is fairly made to palpitate by the luscious
strains of the modern waltz.   Her soul is carried
swooning along, over waves of syrup; she seems to
breathe an atmosphere heavy with ambergris and
musk. From the jolly little thing it was at its birth,
the waltz has grown into the voluptuous, heart-
stirring affair with which we are now familiar.

And what has happened to the waltz has happened to all popular music.   It was once innocent
but is now provocative ;   once pellucid, now
richly clotted ;   once elegant, now deliberately
barbarous.   Compare the music of *The Beggar's
Opera* with the music of a contemporary revue.
They differ as life in the garden of Eden differed
from life in the artistic quarter of Gomorrah. The
one is prelapsarian in its airy sweetness, the other
is rich, luscious and loud with conscious savagery.

The evolution of popular music has run parallel
on a lower plane, with the evolution of serious

music. The writers of popular tunes are not musicians enough to be able to invent new forms of expression. All they do is to adapt the discoveries of original geniuses to the vulgar taste. Ultimately and indirectly, Beethoven is responsible for all the languishing waltz tunes, all the savage jazzings, for all that is maudlin and violent in our popular music. He is responsible because it was he who first devised really effective musical methods for the direct expression of emotion. Beethoven's emotions happened to be noble ; moreover, he was too intellectual a musician to neglect the formal, architectural side of music. But unhappily he made it possible for composers of inferior mind and character to express in music their less exalted passions and vulgarer emotions. He made possible the weakest sentimentalities of Schumann, the baroque grandiosities of Wagner, the hysterics of Scriabine ; he made possible the waltzes of all the Strausses, from the *Blue Danube* to the waltz from *Salome*. And he made possible, at a still further remove, such masterpieces of popular art as ' You made me love you ' and ' That coal black mammy of mine.'

For the introduction of a certain vibrant sexual quality into music, Beethoven is perhaps less directly responsible than the nineteenth-century

Italians. I used often to wonder why it was that Mozart's operas were less popular than those of Verdi, Leoncavallo and Puccini. You couldn't ask for more, or more infectiously 'catchy' tunes than are to be found in *Figaro* or *Don Giovanni*. The music though 'classical,' is not obscure, nor forbiddingly complex. On the contrary it is clear, simple with that seemingly easy simplicity which only consummate genius can achieve and thoroughly engaging. And yet for every time *Don Giovanni* is played, *La Bohème* is played a hundred. *Tosca* is at least fifty times as popular as *Figaro*. And if you look through a catalogue of gramophone records you will find that, while you can buy *Rigoletto* complete in thirty discs, there are not more than three records of *The Magic Flute*. This seems at first sight extremely puzzling. But the reason is not really far to seek. Since Mozart's day composers have learned the art of making music throatily and palpitatingly sexual. The arias of Mozart have a beautiful clear purity which renders them utterly insipid compared with the sobbing, catch-in-the-throaty melodies of the nineteenth-century Italians. The public, having accustomed itself to this stronger and more turbid brewage, finds no flavour in the crystal songs of Mozart.

No essay on modern popular music would be complete without some grateful reference to Rossini, who was, so far as I know, the first composer to show what charms there are in vulgar melody. Melodies before Rossini's day were often exceedingly commonplace and cheap ; but almost never do they possess that almost indefinable quality of low vulgarity which adorns some of the most successful of Rossini's airs, and which we recognize as being somehow a modern, contemporary quality. The methods which Rossini employed for the achievement of his melodic vulgarity are not easy to analyse. His great secret, I fancy, was the very short and easily memorable phrase frequently repeated in different parts of the scale. But it is easiest to define by example. Think of Moses' first Aria in *Moses in Egypt*. That is an essentially vulgar melody ; and it is quite unlike the popular melodies of an earlier date. Its affinities are with the modern popular tune. It is to his invention of vulgar tunes that Rossini owed his enormous contemporary success. Vulgar people before his day had to be content with Mozart's delicate airs. Rossini came and revealed to them a more congenial music. That the world fell down and gratefully worshipped him is not surprising. If he has long ceased to be popular, that is because his successors, profiting by his lessons, have achieved in his own vulgar line triumphs of which he could not have dreamed.

Barbarism has entered popular music from two sources—from the music of barbarous people, like the negroes, and from serious music which has drawn upon barbarism for its inspiration. The technique of being barbarous effectively has come, of course, from serious music. In the elaboration of this technique no musicians have done more than the Russians. If Rimsky-Korsakoff had never lived, modern dance music would not be the thing it is.

Whether, having grown inured to such violent and purely physiological stimuli as the clashing and drumming, the rhythmic throbbing and wailing glissandos of modern jazz music can supply, the world will ever revert to something less crudely direct, is a matter about which one cannot prophesy. Even serious musicians seem to find it hard to dispense with barbarism. In spite of the monotony and the appalling lack of subtlety which characterize the process, they persist in banging away in the old Russian manner, as though there were nothing more interesting or exciting to be thought of. When, as a boy, I first heard Russian music, I was carried off my feet by its wild melodies, its persistent, its relentlessly throbbing rhythms. But my excitement grew less and less with every hearing. To-day no music seems to me more tedious. The only music a civilized man can take unfailing pleasure in is civilized music. If you were compelled to listen every day of your life to a single piece of music, would you choose Stravinsky's ' Oiseau de Feu' or Beethoven's 'Grosse Fugue'? Obviously, you would choose the fugue, if only for its intricacy and because there is more in it to occupy the mind than in the Russian's too simple rhythms. Composers seem to forget that we are, in spite of everything and though appearances may be against us, tolerably civilized. They overwhelm us not merely with Russian and negroid noises, but with Celtic caterwaulings on the black notes, with dismal Spanish wailings, punctuated by the rattle of the castanets and the clashing harmonies of the guitar. When serious composers have gone back to civilized music—and already some of them are turning from barbarism—we shall probably hear a corresponding change for the more refined in popular music. But until serious musicians lead the way, it will be absurd to expect the vulgarizers to change their style.

THE MYSTERY OF THE
THEATRE

ONCE, in the course of an ill-spent life, it was my fate to go to the theatre some two hundred and fifty times in one year. On business, I need not add ; one would hardly do that sort of thing for pleasure. I was paid to go.

By the end of the year—and, for that matter, long before our planet had completed its orbit round the sun—I had come to the conclusion that I was not paid enough ; that, indeed, I could never be paid enough for this particular job. I gave it up ; and nothing would now induce me to resume it.

Since then, my attendances at the theatre have averaged perhaps three per annum.

And yet there are people who go to every first night, not because they have to, not because the griping belly must be filled, but because they like it. They are not paid to go ; they pay, as though for a privilege. The ways of men are indeed strange.

Concerning this mystery, I used often to speculate—abstracting myself as completely as I could from the environing horrors—during the most excruciating passages of the plays which I had to attend. Sitting all round me in the stalls—it was

253

thus I used to reflect—are several hundred prosperous and, as education goes, well-educated people, who have paid money to see this drivelling play (for I am assuming that the play is one of the nineteen drivelling ones and not the rare twentieth *Heartbreak House* or *At Mrs. Beam's*). They are the sort of people who, in the privacy of their homes, would read the better class of novels, or at any rate not the worst. They would be indignant if you offered them a penny novelette.

And yet these readers of respectable fiction will go to the theatre (under no compulsion, be it remembered) to see plays which, as literature, are precisely on a level with the penny novelettes they scorn, very rightly and naturally, to read.

In their novels they demand a certain minimum of probability, truth to life, credible characterization and decent writing. An impossible story, in which the personages are so many dolls, moving in obedience to the laws of an absurd and outworn convention and expressing themselves in a grotesque, tumid and ungrammatical English—this would disgust them. But to a play answering precisely to this description, they will flock in their thousands. They will be moved to tears and enthusiasm by situations which, in a novel, they would find merely ludicrous. They will let pass, and even fervidly admire, language which any one with the slightest feeling for the use of words would shudder to see in print.

It was over this strange anomaly that I used to ponder during those hideous evenings at the theatre. Why does the penny novelette disgust, in book form, those who delight in it when exhibited on the stage ? Put succinctly, that was the not uninteresting problem.

Mr. Bernard Shaw has said that it is easier to write a novel than a play ; and to show with what horrible facility a novelist can spin out into pages of thin description what the dramatist must compress into a few lines of dialogue, he re-wrote in modern narrative form a scene from *Macbeth*. Admittedly, Shakespeare stood the comparison very well. For it is certainly easier to write a bad novel than a good play. But on the other hand, it is much easier to write a bad play that will be successful—even with a quite intelligent and discriminating audience—than a bad novel that will take in readers of the same class. A dramatist can ' get away with ' a play in which there is no characterization subtler than caricature, no beauty of language less coarse than ranting rhetoric, no resemblance to life—only an effective situation. The novelist cannot.

This fact was recently impressed upon me (yet once more) when I went to the theatre in Parma —not, alas, the great Estensian theatre, but a gimcrack little modern playhouse—to see the Italian version of one of Sir Arthur Pinero's plays —*His House in Order* it is called, if I remember rightly, in English. I confess that I thoroughly enjoyed the performance. English *Higlif*, as seen through the eyes of an Italian touring company was worth coming far—all the way from England—to study. And the comedians were admirable. But I marvelled, as I listened, that a piece so entirely empty—for at Parma the unconscious humour and the good acting were merely accidental additions to the blank original —could have been, could still be, such a success. And as a hard-working novelist, I envied the lucky playwrights who can turn out a popular and even highly esteemed piece, in which the personages are either wooden puppets or caricatures, the language rant, and the plot a succession of those cheap epigrams of circumstance known as 'situations.' If I were allowed to make a novel out of only these ingredients, I should congratulate myself on having got off uncommonly cheaply.

What makes it possible for the dramatist to put

so little into his plays, and yet successfully 'get away with it,' is, of course, the intervention of living interpreters.   If he knows the trick—and one learns by practice—the dramatist can pass on to the actor the greater part of his responsibilities. All that he need do, if he is lazy, is to invent effective situations and leave the actors to make the most of them.   Characterization, truth to life, ideas, decent writing and all the rest, he can resign to the writers for print, secure in the knowledge that the public will be too much taken up with the antics of the players to remark the absence of these merely literary trifles.

For it is the players, of course, who reconcile an otherwise relatively discriminating public to the sad stuff which finds its way on to the stage. It is for the sake of the comedians that occupants of the stalls who might, if they were sitting by their own firesides, be reading, shall we say, Wells or Conrad, or D. H. Lawrence, or even Dostoievsky, are content to put up with the dramatic equivalent of the penny novelette and the picture-paper serial story ; for the sake of the living, smiling comedians ; for the personal touch, the palpitating human note.

If acting were always first class, I could understand people becoming hardened first-nighters—

or shouldn't one rather say 'softened'? for the contemporary theatre is more relaxing than tonic, more emollient than astringent—becoming, then, softened first-nighters. A fine piece of acting is as well worth looking at as a fine performance in any other branch of art.

But good actors are as rare as good painters or good writers. Not more than two or three of the very best appear in every generation. I have seen a few. Old Guitry, for example. And Marie Lloyd, the marvellous, rich, Shakespearean Marie, now dead—alas, too soon ; *car elle était du monde où les plus belles choses ont le pire destin.* And Little Tich. And Raquel Meller, marvellous both as diseuse and cinema actress, the most refined, the most nobly aristocratic interpreter of passion I have ever seen ; *une âme bien née* if ever there was one. And Charlie Chaplin. All men and women of genius.

Such perfect performances as theirs are of course worth watching. And there are plenty of smaller talents, not to be despised. I am as willing to pay money to see these comedians interpreting nonsense as to pay to see a good play badly acted (and it is extraordinary how actor-proof a really good play can be). But why any one should pay to see a poor, or even very com-